CRUSH THE IRS

50 INCREDIBLE TAX-SAVING BUSINESS STRATEGIES

IT'S YOUR MONEY!
KEEP IT
OR
GIVE IT TO THE IRS!

First Edition

David C. Zubler, EA

Important Notice

While every effort has been taken to ensure that the information contained herein is accurate as of the time of publication, tax laws and regulations are continually changing.

This book is designed to provide accurate information in regard to the subject matter. However, it is only intended to make you aware of basic tax information. It is not designed to provide you with every intricate detail and every possible scenario concerning each issue. The author and publisher expressly disclaim any and all liability to any persons whatsoever in respect of anything done by any such person in reliance, whether in whole or in part, on this book.

Any services, references, and/or websites that may be mentioned or referred to in this manual are provided for information purposes only. Please take appropriate legal and/or professional advice before acting on any information in this manual.

If a tax issue applies to you, you need to research the topic thoroughly, or contact a competent tax professional, to ensure that you have all the necessary details. If expert assistance is required, the services of a qualified tax professional should be used. The publisher does not guarantee or warrant that readers who use the information provided in this book would get results similar to those discussed.

DEDICATION

I would like to dedicate this book to the Ruth Zubler Boyer Foundation, a charitable Foundation that I created to help underprivileged children. All of my book proceeds go to the Ruth Zubler Boyer Foundation. For more information about the Foundation, go to my website, YourTaxCare.com.

ACKNOWLEDGEMENTS

I want to thank my very beautiful wife, Brenda, who supported me while I dedicated all my free time to writing this book.

I want to thank Greg Romsdal, Lance Fountaine, Tom Zubler, and Jeff Stachowski for their advice and assistance in creating this book.

I want to thank the very talented artists Jim Bright and Alison Oakes Corle for their assistance in designing the cover.

I want to thank my producer Mark Hodgen for doing an outstanding job producing my One-Minute Tax Tip radio show.

I want to thank my amazing voice coach Roger Love for helping me become a much more effective communicator for my presentations, radio program, and television interviews.

I want to thank Yellow Submarine Coaching for teaching me how to get more of what I want out of life.
yellowsubmarinecoachingllc.com

FORWARD

I want to make the readers aware of some tax strategies which may save them a considerable amount of money on their taxes each year. I also want to share strategies that provide other benefits such as writing off vacations, cabins, beach house, and second homes. I also want to help the readers avoid potential problems with the IRS.

This book is intended to provide the readers with valuable concepts that they can easily grasp and benefit from as quickly as possible. Consequently, I wanted to avoid going into great detail and overwhelming the readers with complex information and technical jargon.

If you find a topic in this book that is relevant to you, be sure to research the issue further. You can study the information in IRS Publications or contact competent tax professionals for more detailed information. You can also go to my website for additional information from my newspaper columns, radio interviews, and videos.

Tax laws are always changing. If you would like to stay current, my website will also provide some of the more useful updates on the most recent tax changes that will be beneficial to most people.

Find my latest updates at YourTaxCare.com

Also, if you have questions, you can send me an email at: David@YourTaxCare.com and I will get back to you as soon as possible.

INTRODUCTION

Hello, my name is David Zubler, and I would like to share a little about myself.

My passion is helping people in as many ways as possible.

I'm an Enrolled Agent and the founder and president of Your Tax Care. We provide tax news, services, and education for everyone at YourTaxCare.com.

I'm the author of 6 tax books, a syndicated newspaper columnist, have a daily radio program, and have appeared on national television. My newspaper columns and radio programs are available on the website.

This book includes 50 of my favorite business tax strategies along with 5 bonus strategies. I hope this book will provide you with several strategies that save you money and provide you with valuable information.

I receive a great deal of satisfaction from saving people money and helping people with their tax problems. When you have rescued extremely stressed and despondent clients from their overwhelming problems with IRS, and they say things like "you saved my house and marriage", "you brought me tears of joy", and "you're a godsend," it gives me an incredible feeling that I am serving my life's purpose.

All of my Amazon proceeds from my 6 books go directly to a charitable foundation that I created for underprivileged children. The foundation's purpose is to provide food, clothing, books, medical treatment, and scholarships for underprivileged children. I grew up in a relatively low-income family. Fortunately, I had an aunt who was a schoolteacher who helped to support my brothers and me. If it weren't for her, I wouldn't be where I am today. My mission is to have the same effect that she had on me for as many kids as possible

I have been very blessed with an opportunity to help others.

Additional tax strategies, tax news, and valuable information are available on my videos, radio shows, and newspaper columns at YourTaxCare.com.

For questions or if you are interested in our services, I can be contacted by call or text at (865) 221-7477 or email at David@YourTaxCare.com

CONTENTS

and Build Wealth

Bonus Chapters

Chapter 1

Hire Your Spouse

Hiring your spouse as an employee can save a substantial amount of money on your taxes. This is especially true if you are a sole proprietor or if you have a single-member LLC.

Your spouse may be able to help you take care of bookkeeping or running errands.

You may be able to save thousands of dollars a year without spending any additional money.

You will receive no tax savings from paying your spouse by cash wages. Doing this would essentially just be moving income from one place on your tax return to another.

If you want to save money you need to pay your spouse with as many tax-free employee benefits as possible.

Employee benefits like health insurance, life insurance and medical reimbursement plans aren't taxable income for your spouse-employee, but they are a deductible expense for you as an employer.

Deducting these employee benefits can provide huge tax savings. Health benefits generally provide the largest tax-free fringe benefit for saving on taxes. Deducting your spouse's benefits not only reduces your taxable income, but they also reduce your self-employment taxes as well.

The plan for deducting health insurance is very simple. Your spouse buys a health insurance plan in their name that covers the entire family (including you). Since you are the employer, you can reimburse your spouse for the health insurance premiums.

You can also reimburse your spouse for health expenses which are not covered by the insurance. This includes deductibles, copays and prescriptions for everyone in your family. This allows you to reimburse your spouse for essentially all your medical expenses.

Other tax-free employee benefits that are allowable for your spouse include the cost of a smartphone, job-related education and de minimis fringe benefits. De minimis fringe benefits include relatively low-cost expenditures such as occasional meals, small gifts, sporting event or theater tickets, and flowers or fruit on special occasions.

However, you need to know the rules and how to take advantage of the rules to save as much as possible. But it is also extremely important to keep it from backfiring on you from not going by the rules.

It is extremely important to make sure your wife is your bona fide employee. The IRS may try to claim that your spouse is not a bona fide employee. If the IRS is successful, you would lose out on your tax savings and pay a substantial amount of penalties and interest.

Make sure that you follow these rules when hiring your
2

spouse:
- Your spouse cannot be a co-owner of the business. This would turn the business into a partnership which wouldn't work.

- Your spouse must perform actual work for your business.

- Keep track of the work your spouse performs, and the hours worked by having them fill out a weekly time sheet.

- You must make the management decisions and your spouse must work under your control.

- Your spouse should pay all medical expenses from their separate bank account.

- Your spouse's compensation must be reasonable. Avoid overpaying your spouse for their services.

- Hiring your spouse can legally save a substantial amount of money in taxes when done correctly.

Chapter 2

Hire Your Children

Paying your kids to work for you can provide substantial tax savings. It also provides your children with an opportunity to learn the business and to see your work ethic. It can help your child pay for college, or you can put it into their retirement account.

Your kids may be able to help you take care of bookkeeping or running errands.

Kids under age 18 who work for their parents are not subject to Social Security and Medicare taxes if the business is taxed as a sole proprietorship or a partnership in which the father and mother are the only partners. If your business is a single-member LLC and is taxed as a proprietorship or as a spouse-only partnership, you will also be able to take advantage of not paying payroll taxes. Since corporations don't qualify as mothers and fathers of the children, they don't qualify for this tax savings.

The standard deduction for a single person in 2019 is $12,200, so they would not be subject to income taxes until their income exceeded this amount. Additionally, up to $5,500 can be put into an IRA. If your child makes more than their standard deduction, putting money into their IRA would increase the amount of tax-free wages.

4

Child wages are only deductible if the pay is a reasonable amount, actually paid, and based on actual services provided by the child. There is no minimum age for the child, and the IRS has approved the hiring of a seven-year-old in the Eller case.

The kiddie tax is not an issue because it only applies to unearned income.

The Fair Labor Standards Act allows kids younger than 16 who work in a business solely owned by their parents to work at any time of day and for any number of hours.

An employer with employees is required to have an employer ID number. If you don't already have one you can apply for an employer ID online on the IRS website.

It's essential to have your child complete a timesheet daily and turn it in weekly, to avoid having the IRS disallow the wages.

You should always pay wages using a W-2 payroll check. You will also need to be able to provide an audit trail from your business checkbook to your child's bank account since this is now your child's money. If you are using a payroll service, be sure to explain your child is exempt from payroll taxes and then check to make sure they are doing it correctly.

It is essential to file all federal and state forms which are required. The required forms include the W-4, W-2, quarterly Form 941, and annual Form 940.

Failure to fill out all payroll records and forms can have significant consequences. The IRS can disallow the wage deduction, and you can be required to pay negligence penalties.

Chapter 3

Rent From Your Spouse

Renting from your spouse reduces self-employment tax. If you are a sole proprietor, the 15.3% self-employment can quickly increase your tax liability. However, you may be able to use a simple strategy to reduce your taxes. If you own an office building or other assets, you can create a rental arrangement with your spouse that could substantially reduce your self-employment taxes.

A sole proprietorship's income is reported on Schedule C and is subject to self-employment tax.

If you have a sole proprietorship and you earn $100,000 of net income, your self-employment tax liability would be $14,130.

Rental income is reported on Schedule E and is not subject to self-employment tax.

This is how the rental strategy can reduce your self-employment tax. You give an office building to your spouse. Your spouse then rents the office space back to you.

However, to do this, you will need a valid non-tax purpose for the transaction, which will be explained later. You pay your spouse $2,000 rent monthly (the fair rental

7

value of the building), which takes $24,000 off Schedule C and onto Schedule E. Schedule E, unlike Schedule C, does not create self-employment taxes. So, this strategy reduces your self-employment income by $24,000, which saves you $3,391.

The IRS will not accept this strategy unless you can show a valid business or non-tax purpose for the leaseback and transfer of your property.

Business owners often put their real estate in a separate LLC for liability protection reasons. The IRS accepts that liability protection is a common and legitimate reason to create a self-rental arrangement.

Another example of why you might transfer the property is to ensure that your spouse has a separate income stream. This would also provide the right to take out loans on the property and sell the property in case your spouse needed money.

There is no gift tax, estate tax, or income tax consequences when you give property to your spouse.

However, you should take into consideration that giving your spouse complete ownership of your business property may have negative consequences outside of tax, such as in a divorce proceeding.

It's important to go through all the formalities of the lease contract that you enter into with your spouse. These formalities are provided below.

Create documentation at the time of the transaction,

which explains your business and personal reasons for transferring your property to your spouse.

You are required to treat the lease as if you were renting from someone unrelated, and your spouse must act as though he or she is the owner of the property.

You will need to find the fair rental value of the property and avoid paying no more or less than this amount, taking into consideration your ownership in the property.

You will need to create a written lease agreement. Lease agreement templates can be found online.

You will need to make actual payments to your spouse, and your spouse should deposit the money into a separate checking account for the rental property.

Your spouse will need to pay all expenses and debts relating to the property. However, if you have ownership in the property, you will pay your share of the expenses and debts.

You will need to give your spouse a Form 1099-MISC for the rent that you paid during the year, regardless of whose name is on the title.

If you reside in one of the community property states, you must take steps to give your spouse 100% ownership of the asset. The community property states are Arizona, California, Idaho, Louisiana, Nevada, New Mexico, Texas, Washington, and Wisconsin.

You can also use self-rental if you co-own property with your spouse. Self-rental is allowed even though you and your spouse file a joint tax return. However, the amount of tax savings is reduced by 50% as compared to when your spouse is the sole owner. This is because you can deduct rent from Schedule C only for payments relating to property that you do not own.

The renting from your spouse strategy works by moving your income from your Schedule C, which has self-employment tax and onto your joint return Schedule E, which does not.

Chapter 4

Turn Your Husband-Wife Partnership into and S Corporation

If you and your spouse currently have a husband-wife partnership, changing the entity to an S corporation could result in a sizable tax savings.

When you are a partner in a partnership, you are required to pay self-employment tax on your share of the profit. The self-employment tax is the government's way of collecting Social Security and Medicare taxes from the partners since the taxes aren't taken out as they would be if they were employees.

The self-employment tax consists of the 12.4% Social Security tax on the first $147,000 (the ceiling in 2022) of net self-employment income plus the 2.9% Medicare tax. The 2.9% Medicare tax component continues before increasing to 3.8% as a result of the 0.9% additional Medicare tax.

If your net self-employment income surpasses the $147,000 Social Security tax ceiling, the Social Security tax part of the self-employment tax reaches the ceiling and the tax ends.

The self-employment tax for husband-wife partners is a double whammy since they are both required to pay the tax. If you and your spouse each have net self-employment income of $137,700 from your partnership your combined self-employment tax is $42,136.

Converting your partnership into an S corporation and set your salaries at $50,000 would be a huge reduction in your self-employment taxes. Converting would reduce the FICA tax bill to only $15,300 ($50,000 x 15.3% x 2 =$15,300). This would result in a savings of $22,950 in Social Security and Medicare taxes by operating as an S corporation ($15,300 versus $38,250).

The IRS knows about the strategy of using low salaries for S corporation shareholder-employees to reduce payroll taxes. If the IRS audits your corporation, they may attempt to prove that the cash distributions paid to you were simply disguised salary payments if your salary is too low. If the IRS succeeds in winning their claim, your S corporation will be assessed back FICA taxes, interest, and penalties.

Consequently, you should be able to defend your salaries as being reasonable for the work you are doing. However, it is to your benefit to have salaries which are on the low side of the reasonable salary range. If your salaries are in the reasonable range the IRS will be less inclined to contest it.

You are not likely to lose the battle with the IRS if you can demonstrate that outsiders could be hired to perform your job for a similar salary. Consequently, it's important to be knowledgeable about the salary and be able to support your case.

The ability to accurately estimate the amount of your
12

future tax savings from converting to an S corporation depends on your ability to project the amount of future business profit.

Chapter 5

Use Family Limited Partnerships to Reduce Your Taxes

This strategy involves using a Family Limited Partnership (FLP) to transfer income to your children or other family members who are taxed at a lower rate. However, it can also be used to transfer assets to family members

A family limited partnership (FLP) is owned by family members and abides by the rules of a limited partnership. Parents often form an FLP and for the purpose of transferring their assets, such as an existing business, to this entity. However, a business can be formed as an FLP from the start.

An FLP is often used to shift present business income to lower-bracket family members. The parents are the general partners, and the children are the limited partners. In this scenario, the children have no right to manage or make decisions for the business. They are simply treated like investors who have an ownership interest in the business only. Each child can receive a limited partnership interest worth $32,000 each year (2022 figure) ($16,000 from each parent) as gifts without federal gift and estate tax consequences to anyone (there may be state gift tax consequences). Gift and estate tax imposed on gifts in excess of the annual gift tax exclusion may also be offset by your applicable exclusion amount to the extent that is available. Limited partners can work in the business and be compensated for their services.

The annual gift tax exclusion is indexed for inflation and increases periodically.

If you make gifts of interests in a family partnership to family members, allocations of partnership income (this does not include compensation for services they provide to the partnership) to such family members is not allowed unless capital is a material income-producing factor in the partnership. Even when capital is a material income-producing factor, special rules may limit the amount of income that can be allocated to such family members.

Be careful of the kiddie tax. This law was created to discourage wealthier individuals from transferring assets to their children to take advantage of their lower tax rates. The current rules tax a minor child's unearned income including capital gains distributions, dividends, and interest income—at the parents' tax rate if it exceeds the annual limit of $2,200 in 2021 and $2,300 in 2022.

The tax applies to dependent children under the age of 18 at the end of the tax year (or full-time students younger than 24) and works like this:

The first $1,100 of unearned income that is covered by the kiddie tax isn't taxed due to the kiddie tax's standard deduction.

The next $1,100 is taxed at the child's marginal tax rate.

Any income exceeding $2,200 is taxed at the parents' marginal tax rate.
15

If your child has income from a job the rules become more complex.

The kiddie tax doesn't apply in certain situations. If your child is age 18 or over, if your child's earned income doesn't exceed one-half of his or her support, the kiddie tax does not apply. If your child is age 24 or over if your child is a full-time student and your child's earned income doesn't exceed one-half of his or her support), however, and gets unearned income from the family partnership, the kiddie tax doesn't apply. The kiddie tax doesn't apply if your child is 24 or older and is a full-time student and your child's income doesn't exceed half of their support.

It is also possible to minimize Social Security payroll/self-employment taxes by restructuring your business entity. Limited partners don't pay self-employment tax on their distributive share of partnership income. However, they do pay self-employment tax on guaranteed payments.

Guaranteed payments are payments made by a partnership to a partner that are determined without regard to the partnership's income. A partnership treats guaranteed payments for services, or for the use of capital, as if they were made to a person who is not a partner.

FLPs have many features that can result in significant tax savings. Consequently, the IRS has begun to examine them more closely to make sure that the business is abiding by the rules. The rules are too complex to include in this book. If you are considering creating a FLP, it's critical to consult a tax professional to gain thorough knowledge of the rules.

Chapter 6

Benefits of a Home Office

Small business owners may qualify for a home office deduction that will help them save money on their taxes.

Many people are unaware of one particular tax benefit that an office in the home provides. If you have an office in your home that qualifies as a principal place of business, you can deduct your daily transportation costs between your home and another work location in the same trade or business (See Pub. 587). If you don't claim an office in your home, some of your work mileage will be considered commuting mileage, which is nondeductible. When you have an office in your home, all of your work-related mileage is tax- deductible. The additional business mileage can have a significant impact on saving taxes.

Taxpayers can take this deduction if they use a portion of their home exclusively, and on a regular basis, for any of the following:

As the taxpayer's main place of business.

As a place of business where the taxpayer meets patients, clients, or customers, the taxpayer must meet these people in the normal course of business.

If it is a separate structure that is not attached to the taxpayer's home. The taxpayer must use this structure in connection with their business.

A place where the taxpayer stores inventory or samples. This place must be the sole, fixed location of their business.

Under certain circumstances, the structure where the taxpayer provides daycare services.

Deductible expenses for business use of a home include real estate taxes, mortgage interest, rent, utilities, insurance, depreciation, repairs and maintenance, and casualty losses.

Certain expenses are limited to the net income of the business. These are known as allocable expenses. They include things such as utilities, insurance, and depreciation. While allocable expenses cannot create a business loss, they can be carried forward to the next year. If the taxpayer carries them forward, the expenses are subject to the same limitation rules.

There are two options for figuring and claiming the home office deduction.

Regular method

This method requires dividing the above expenses of operating the home between personal and business use. Self-employed taxpayers compute this deduction on Form 8829.

Simplified method
18

The simplified method reduces the paperwork and record-keeping for small businesses. The simplified method has a set rate of $5 a square foot for business use of the home. The maximum deduction allowed is based on up to 300 square feet.

There are special rules for certain business owners:

- Daycare providers complete a special worksheet, which is found in Publication 587.

- Self-employed individuals use Form 1040 and Schedule C to claim the deduction.

- Farmers frequently overlook this deduction. Farmers claim this deduction on Schedule F, Line 32.

Chapter 7

Deducting Business Use of Your Garage

Claiming a deduction for business use of a garage can provide you with additional tax savings. Taking the deduction for several years can result in significant savings.

A garage can be deducted for various reasons, including manufacturing goods, storing equipment and inventory.

There are different methods for calculating business use of the home. To get the maximum deduction, you should calculate the business percentage for each option and then use the largest business percentage option.

You can calculate business use of the home by dividing the actual dimensions of the area used for business by the total square footage of your home.

Another option for calculating business use of the home is by the number of rooms.

If the rooms in your home are similar in size, you can calculate the business percentage by dividing the number of rooms used for business by the total number of rooms in your home. If your garage is considerably larger than most of the rooms in your house, your garage may need to be counted as more than one room.

The IRS has different rules for a detached garage. To deduct an office, you are not required to meet the strict tests for a principal place of business or the alternative test for a place to see clients or customers. Fortunately, the test to claim an office in a detached garage is simply to determine that it's used in the normal course of business. However, to eliminate commuting miles, you need the home office to be your principal place of business. Eliminating commuting miles provides the most significant tax savings for many businesses.

If you don't have an office in your home, the IRS requires you to determine commuting and business miles. When you leave home, the first stop of the day is commuting miles. Your drive from the last business location to your home would also be commuting miles. As an example, suppose a salesman visited five clients. The trip from his home to his first client would be commuting.

You would also consider the trip from the last client to home commuting miles which is not deductible.

If part of your home is not usable, it is more advantageous not to include it as part of your total home square footage for the business of the home calculation. For instance, an attic without a floor should not be used as part of the total square footage of your home. This would reduce the total square footage of your home and increase your business use of home percentage. If you are using an attic for business but not the garage, you would want to claim the garage is not usable space.

Chapter 8

Sell Fixer-upper Houses and Pay No Taxes

You can avoid paying income taxes on the gain of a fixer-upper house. This strategy involves taking advantage of the tax-free gain on the sale of a home. For people who love to work on houses, this can be a great way to make money and pay no taxes.

This strategy requires that you live in the house for 2 of the last 5 years. The tax-free gain is up to $500,000 for couples and $250,000 for singles. The tax-free gain is a lifetime gain. As an example, if you are married, you could sell 5 houses with gains of $100,000 before paying any taxes.

Normally the gain is not reported on your tax return if it is a tax-free sale of home gain. However, if the sale is reported to the IRS on a Form 1099-S, Proceeds from Real Estate Transactions, you will need to report the sale on your tax return. Since you received a Form 1099-S for the sale, the sale should be reported on Form 8949 and Schedule D in your tax return. The sales price and cost basis will be the same amount, which will result in no gain.

If you have never flipped houses, you will need to have some crucial knowledge before jumping in.

It's crucial that the real estate contract include an

22

inspection clause.

To be successful with this strategy, you will need to be able to accurately estimate a purchase price that will provide the profit that you desire. This requires calculating the cost to repair the house and its likely market value after the renovation. Start by adding up the costs to renovate the property based on a thorough assessment of the condition of the house, including materials and labor. Include another 5 to 10% for unforeseen problems.

Remodeling a fixer-upper can cost a lot of money, so it's critical you have the right financing lined up. Some home renovation mortgages allow you to roll remodeling costs into your loan amount with a single mortgage.

These programs include the Fannie Mae HomeStyle Loan, Freddie Mac's CHOICERenovation Mortgage, FHA 203(k) loan, and VA renovation loan.

One problem that you may encounter with this strategy is that a lot of lenders are wary of approving mortgages on houses in poor condition to people without great credit. One way to get around this is to buy the home financed by the seller. This way, you also avoid any hassles with mortgage companies, and you can negotiate the interest rate with the seller.

This IRS rule allows you to repeat this process every two years, keeping all that tax-free income over and over.

Selling fixer-upper homes can enable you to make hundreds of thousands of dollars in profits while avoiding paying tens of thousands of dollars in taxes.

Chapter 9

Make Installment Sales to Increase Profits, Reduce Taxes, and Build Wealth

If you sell your home, rental property, investment property or flip house, you should consider an installment sale and seller financing.

This strategy is an excellent method for increasing your profits and building wealth.

Seller financing allows you to earn more interest than you would otherwise. People who are looking for seller financing are generally unable to get a mortgage through a bank for several reasons. They may not have the cash they need to close on a home or rental property.

Consequently, they are often willing to pay a higher price for the property and a higher interest. The higher price results in a larger profit. The higher interest rates enable you to have passive earnings for additional profit while accumulating a substantial amount of wealth.

In the event that you have to repossess the property, you keep the cash you've collected and keep the property. This allows you to sell the property again. In fact, many investors hope that they are able to foreclose.

Installment sales can substantially reduce your capital gains tax and in some cases, you can completely avoid

24

capital gains. The reason for this is that the capital gains rate can be as low as 0%.

The capital gains rate depends on your taxable income. The higher your income, the higher the rate.

Currently, if you sell a property that you held for at least one year, any gain from the sale is taxed at either a 0%, 15% or 20% rate.

For a single person, the 2021 capital gains rate is:

- Income between $0 and $40,400 rate is 0%.

- Income between $40,001 and $445,850 rate is 15%.

- Income over $445,850 rate is 20%

For a single person, the 2022 capital gains rate is:

- Income between $0 and $41,676 rate is 0%.

- Income between $41,676 and $459,750 rate is 15%.

- Income over $459,750 rate is 20%

As an example of how the taxes are reduced, Jeremy is single and has wages of $47,000 in 2021. His taxable income after the standard deduction is $34,600. His tax would be $4,020.

He decides to sell a property for a gain of $100,000. However, he does an installment sale over 20 years and reports a gain of $5,000 each year. His capital gains tax rate would be 0%. Consequently, his tax at the end of the
25

year would still be $4,020 and he would pay no taxes on the capital gains.

However, if he had decided to sell the property without making an installment sale his tax would be $18,148. Consequently, he would be paying $14,128 in capital gains tax. If he had done an installment sale over 20 years, he would have saved $14,128 in taxes.

Special rules apply when selling a rental property to your relatives. If you sell a depreciable property (rental property) on an installment contract to your relative, and they sell it within two years of buying it, you are treated as receiving a payment equal to what your relative received. Avoid selling a rental property to a relative.

Installment sales are an excellent way to increase your profit and build wealth while reducing capital gains tax.

Chapter 10

Deduct More Rental Property Losses by Qualifying as a Real Estate Professional

At one time you could invest in rental real estate and take huge tax losses to offset your income. However, Congress passed laws to make it more difficult to take advantage of these losses. This law is known as passive loss rule. When your rental property business or investment is considered a passive activity, you can deduct expenses only to the extent that you have income.

Fortunately, there are strategies that allow you to take these large losses. This requires making your rental property an active (non-passive) business rather than a passive business.

In order to make sure your rental property is active, you will need to show that you qualify as a real estate professional, and you materially participate in the operation of your rental property.

You will qualify as a real estate professional for purposes of the passive loss rules if you meet two requirements.

First, you must perform more than half of your personal services for the year in which you materially participate.

Second, you must perform more than 750 hours of services during the year in "real property trades or

27

businesses."

The 2nd rule that you are required to prove is that you materially participate in the operation of your rental property. You can demonstrate material participation in a property by showing any of the following:

- You worked more than 500 hours on the property.

- You worked over 100 hours on the property & no one worked longer on the property.

- You performed substantially all the work on the property.

You will have to meet the material participation test for each property you own. Material participation is a property-by property rule if you don't group your properties together. You have the option to group your properties all together as if they were a single property.

The grouping election is allowed under IRC §469. The election is a statement that must be attached to your tax return. The election must be filed by the due date of the tax return, including extensions for the year in which the taxpayer wishes to make the election. Once the election is made, you can't change it except for specific circumstances.

If you are married, you can count the material participation labor with your spouse. This will make your rental activity an active business.

It's important to keep good records of your hours worked in case of an audit. In case the IRS investigates, you need to make sure you have documentation to show them.

A rental property can be more than a source of income. It can also be a source for tax deductions to offset your income from other businesses.

You receive the biggest benefit from rental properties appreciated in value but also provide a tax shelter against your other sources of income.

Make your losses deductible by classifying yourself as a real estate professional, and materially participating in each loss-deduction property or group.

Chapter 11

Rent to Your C Corporation for a QBI Deduction

A C corporation is not eligible for the Qualified Business Income (QBI) deduction.

The Tax Care and Job Act (TCJA) lowered the maximum corporate tax rate to 21% to provide tax savings. Other entities were provided with the QBI as a way to lower their taxes, but the C corporation was not.

The QBI deduction can be as much as 20% of taxable income, which can be a considerable tax savings.

Under the right circumstances, an owner of a C corporation can rent a building to the corporation and receive a 20% reduction in taxes on the rental income.

As an example, an owner rents a building to his C corporation and has a $100,000 profit. If the owner meets certain criteria, he can take a 20% QBI deduction and only pay taxes on $80,000 of profit. This would reduce taxable income by $20,000. If the owner is in the 22% tax bracket, this will provide a tax savings of $4,400 from the 20% QBI deduction.

The owner of the building would have to meet the QBI criteria in order to take the 20% deduction. The rental must meet the test as a Section 162 trade or business.

In order to meet the QBI requirements of Section 162, the owner must perform at least 250 hours of rental services each year. This would typically require some time spent doing maintenance in order to meet the 250-hour requirement. Maintenance would include activities such as painting, mowing, and landscaping.

Contemporaneous records of services performed are required to be maintained for tax years beginning after January 1, 2019. According to the IRS, contemporaneous means, the records used to support a claim on your tax return are created and originated at the same time as you claimed the deduction.

Separate books and records must be maintained for the rental activity.

The IRS issued Notice 2019-07, which provides a safe-harbor for a rental real estate activity to qualify as a trade or business for QBI purposes.

A statement signed under penalties of perjury is required to be attached to your tax return that indicates the safe harbor has been satisfied.

The purpose of this chapter is to make you aware of the potential tax savings and provide you with the basic information. However, the QBI requirements of Section 162 are very complex. Additionally, some factors are very subjective, which would require someone with experience to make good judgment decisions. I highly recommend that you contact an expert tax professional if you are interested in taking advantage of this tax strategy.

31

Chapter 12

Vacation Rental Strategies

If you own a rental property and the average rental is seven days or less, the tax code defines it as a vacation hotel of one sort or another.

Providing services for short-term rentals creates a business that is reported on Schedule C Profit or Loss from Business. A business that is reported on Schedule C is subject to self-employment tax in addition to income tax.

Rental properties with an average rental of more than seven days are reported on Schedule E and are not subject to self-employment tax.

Rendering services includes activities such as cleaning linens, washing dishes and maid services. If all you do is clean the lobby, stairways, public entrances and exits, you are not rendering more than occupancy services. In this case, you would report your rental activity on a Schedule E and would not be subject to self-employment tax.

Passive loss rules:

-   For tax purposes regarding the passive loss rules, a property with an average rental of seven days or less is not a rental, even when it is reported on

Schedule E. Consequently, this can have a tax impact on your rental property.

- The tax effect includes the following impact on the passive loss rules:

- It does not qualify for the $25,000 active participation rental loss break.

- It does not produce material participation hours that can be used to become a real estate professional.

- It stands alone under the passive loss rules.

Material participation rules:

- If your rental average is seven days or less and has a loss, you can deduct the loss in the current year only if you materially participate.

- There are tests for material participation regarding the seven days or less rental property.

- Most people will meet one of the two following tests:

- You and your spouse provide substantially all the participation in the rental activity of the property.

- You and your spouse's combined participation exceeds 100 hours, and your hours are more than the participation of any other individual.

Personal use of the property will require you to meet the Section 280A vacation home rules. Do not use the rental for personal purposes without learning these rules.

33

However, you can stay overnight at your rental while you are making repairs.

If you have a profit on your rental, you are likely to have a QBI Section 199A deduction. By meeting the Section 199A requirements, you may be able to deduct 20% of your rental profit.

However, it's a good idea to consult with an expert tax professional since this is a complex issue.

Make sure you keep a record of your hours worked on the property in the event of an audit.

Spending time working on your rental property and meeting the requirements is a strategy that can provide tax benefits.

Chapter 13

Earn Tax-Free Income to Pay for Your Vacation

This strategy enables you to earn passive income to pay for a vacation while on vacation.

The IRS has two for tax-free rental income. It's required to be your residence and rented for less than 15 days in the year.

As long as you meet the two requirements, you don't include the income on your return. Any expenses associated with the rental are not deductible.

If you have more than one residence, each one may qualify for tax-free rental income. The dwelling is considered a residence for the year if you use it for personal purposes more than 14 days or 10% of the days you rent the dwelling.

A dwelling unit includes a house, apartment, condominium, cabin, boat or similar property. However, a dwelling is required to have a sleeping space, toilet and cooking facilities. Consequently, this can limit boat rentals from qualifying as a residence.

Any days that it is rented for less than fair market value count as personal days.

It's very easy to get started renting on Airbnb and the fees are very reasonable. Most property owners pay a flat service fee of 3% of the booking subtotal. Your subtotal is the nightly rate plus your cleaning fee and additional guest fee and doesn't include Airbnb fees and taxes. Guests normally pay a service fee of around 14% of the booking subtotal.

If you are concerned about damage by renters, Airbnb provides free Aircover which provides $1,000,000 liability insurance, damage protection, and pet damage protection.

You may want to check your local regulations before renting your dwelling. In some areas, you are required to register, get a permit, or obtain a license before you list your property or accept guests. Certain types of short-term rentals may be completely prohibited. Local governments vary greatly in how the laws are enforced.

In the event you use a third party to rent your residence, the third party is required to give a 1099-MISC for rents paid if the amount is over $600 for the year. You could also receive a Form-1099K from an online service such as Airbnb. Form-1099K is used to report credit card transactions.

If you receive a Form 1099 or Form-1099K for rental income, you will need to report the income to prevent the IRS from trying to correct your return and including the income. Report the income on Schedule E which is the form used to report rental income and expenses.

Use the "Other Expenses" section of the Schedule E to zero out the income. Enter "Sections 280A(g) Exclusion
36

and the amount of the income.

Renting a residence for less than 15 days does not affect landlords or real estate professionals. This includes real estate professional status, the passive loss rules, or the $25,000 allowed deductions for active real estate rentals. Renting a dwelling can be a great way to make tax-free money to help pay for your vacation while you are on vacation.

Chapter 14

Take Advantage of a Trip that is Business and Personal

This strategy can be very beneficial if you travel for business to look for equipment, attend conventions, or for other business matters.

It is important to know whether you can count your day as a business day and know how to strategize your days to take advantage of a business deduction.

The cost of transportation within the 50 states and Washington, D.C, is either all deductible or nondeductible. If you spend the majority of the trip days on business, you can deduct 100% of your direct-route transportation expenses. If the majority of your days are personal, you get no deduction. Your overnight trip out of town is deductible if its primary purpose is for business.

Generally, this means the majority of the days were for business. There are two types of business days, travel day and presence-required day.

Travel day

The day you spend traveling to your business destination is a travel day, which is deductible. This must be your business destination and not your personal destination.

Presence-required day

If your presence is required at a particular place for a specific and genuine business purpose, it counts as a business day. This would include a meeting with any business associate, employee, partner, customer, or vendor.

You can count a day as a business day when circumstances beyond your control prevent you from pursuing your business objective.

You should take into consideration that if you are on a personal trip and you have a business meeting that takes at least four hours, you can count that entire day as a business day.

You may be able to take advantage of weekends, holidays, and other stand-by days. Weekends, holidays, and other stand-by days sandwiched by business days count as business days when it would not be practical to return home for the weekend. As an example, if you live in Nashville and travel to Los Angeles, it would not be practical or cost- effective to return home for the weekend. However, if you lived in Knoxville and traveled to Nashville, the cost and short drive involved would make it less likely the IRS and the courts would allow it as business days.

If your savings by traveling a day or two earlier or later exceed the cost of traveling the day before or the day after your business function, the extra days would be considered business days.

During your travel, you can deduct the cost of lodging and meals on business days but not personal days. Business-related expenses such as shipping and printing are deductible even on personal days.

If your spouse, dependent, or a friend goes with you, you generally can't deduct their travel expense. However, it may be deductible if it can be adequately shown that their purpose on the trip has a bona fide business purpose.

Example for deducting a vacation

B - Tuesday	fly to location
P – Wednesday	vacation
P - Thursday	vacation
B - Friday	business day for 4 hours
B - Saturday	vacation but business because it's a weekend
B - Sunday	vacation but business because it's a weekend
B - Monday	business day for 4 hours
P - Tuesday	vacation
P - Wednesday	vacation
P - Thursday	vacation
B - Friday	fly home

40

Total business days = 6

Total personal days = 5

You were gone 11 days and worked 2 days and spent 9 days on vacation.

It's a business trip since it has more business days than personal days.

B = Business day

P = Personal day

41

Chapter 15

Live Abroad and Pay No Federal Income Tax on Over $100,000

Imagine living in a dream location abroad and getting a huge tax break on your federal income taxes, or better yet paying no federal income taxes at all.

Additionally, if you qualify for the federal income tax exclusion, you qualify for a housing exclusion of up to 30% of the exempt amount of income.

And if you are married, both of you qualify for the tax breaks.

Both income wages and self-employment income can qualify for the tax breaks for living abroad. This can be a huge savings for a self-employed business owner. The self-employment tax rate is 15.3%, so a self-employed business owner with a profit of $100,000 would save about $15,000 in self-employment taxes in addition to the savings on income taxes.

The amount of the exempt earned income normally increases each year. For 2021 and 2022 the exclusion is $108,700.

To qualify for the foreign earned income exclusion, you need to be a qualified individual and have foreign earned income.

42

A qualified individual must have a tax home in a foreign country and meet one of two residency tests. Your tax home is your regular place of business. To qualify for tax-free income, your tax home must be in a foreign country.

For people with more than one regular place of business, their tax home is at the location that the law rules your principal place of business. To determine your principal place of business you must consider the time spent at each location, business activity at each location, and the financial return from each location.

If you have no principal place of business because of the nature of the business, your residence is the location of your tax home.

You lose your foreign-located tax home for any period that your abode is in the U.S. Your abode is determined by your fixed place of residence.

Having a dwelling in the U.S. does not necessarily mean your abode is in the U.S. Even if your spouse and dependents can live in your home in the U.S. does not mean your abode is in the U.S.

Temporarily living in the U.S. does not necessarily mean that your abode is in the U.S.

To qualify for the foreign earned income exclusion, you must be in a foreign country for 330 full days in a 12-month period.

Foreign income is compensation for services you earn while you have a foreign tax home and meet the
43

residency test. You are required to attribute any income to the year you performed the services. You also need to collect the money before the end of the taxable year following the year the services were performed. For example, if you earned the money in 2022, the money must be collected before 2024.

You will use Form 2555 to claim the foreign earned income exclusion when you file your federal income tax return.

Unless you are living in a country that doesn't have an income tax, you will normally pay income tax in that country. However, there are many nice countries with a tax rate considerably less than the United States. If you operate a business from outside of the U.S., you may be able to avoid the self-employment tax which is a considerable tax savings.

By using the internet and zoom, many small businesses can operate very effectively from another country.

For people who like to travel and see the world, this could be a great opportunity to experience living in another country. Travel by train is very easy and economical in Europe, which would allow you to see many countries while abroad.

Chapter 16

Substantially Increase Your Cruise Deduction

In 1982, the tax law limited the amount of deductions for cruise ship conventions and meetings. Additionally, there were several other limitations. However, you will learn that there is a way for you to avoid the strict rules and limited amount of deductions.

It is important to know the cruise ship deduction rules. The amount of the deduction is limited to $2,000 a year. This includes the cost of the cruise, convention, and travel to get to the cruise port.

The law requires that you attach a signed statement to your tax return. The statement must include your total days on the cruise ship, the hours you devoted to the business activity and the program of the scheduled activities.

To make matters worse, you need to attach to your return a written statement signed by an officer of the sponsoring organization, the daily schedule of business activity and the hours you attended.

The ship must sail under the U.S. flag, and the ports of call are required to be in the United States or its possession.

Fortunately, there is a way to avoid the $2,000 limit and

take a cruise on the ship and the destination you want. This is how it works:

Take a cruise and have a four-hour meeting on land at the last port of call. If the meeting lasts for four hours, the day qualifies as a business day. The days spent traveling from your home to the meeting and the days traveling home after the meeting are travel days. The travel days qualify as business days. Consequently, every day of your trip would be a business day and would be deductible.

By taking the cruise ship to the business meeting and having the meeting on land in the tax-law-defined North American area, you can deduct the entire cost of the convention. This includes the cost of transportation to the cruise port and the cost of the cruise if it is less than the daily luxury water limits. The daily limit is more than the typical cruise ship cost, and you can find the information by googling "daily luxury water limits."

The tax-law-defined North American area includes over 30 islands and countries.

You can google "tax-law-defined North American area" to find all the locations.

For example, you could use this strategy to fly from your home to Miami and stay overnight. Then take a seven-day roundtrip cruise to a Caribbean Island and have a business meeting with your business associates or employees on the last island.

Since the meeting is on land, you are not limited to a U.S possession. If the food is included in the cruise price, you can deduct the entire cost of the cruise. This allows you to deduct the entire cost of the travel, meeting and the cost of the cruise.

This strategy eliminates the $2,000 limit, excessive IRS paperwork requirements, and limited possibilities imposed by the U.S. cruise ship requirement. Fortunately, you can use this strategy to choose any cruise ship and go to destinations in over 30 locations.

Chapter 17

Deduct Travel to an Exotic Location

If you like to travel outside the country, this is a great strategy for you to take advantage of when traveling. The seven-day travel rule allows you to deduct 100% of the transportation cost to a business destination even if you only work one day. You can enjoy spending the rest of your time at the mountains or the beach.

According to Section 274(c)(1), the general rule is if you travel outside of the United States for business purposes, you are entitled to deduct the expense of the travel.

However, you will need to know the two exceptions.

The first exception is that the general rule does not apply when traveling outside the United States when the travel does not exceed one week. You must travel for at least one week. One week means seven consecutive days. You can't include the day that you travel outside the United States. However, you can include the day when the travel ends.

Example:

You leave the United States on a Thursday morning and end the trip the following Thursday afternoon. The IRS considers you to have traveled outside the United States for seven consecutive days. This rule applies when traveling outside the United States only. In this case the rule is defined as the United States and the District of Columbia. Travel to Puerto Rico and the U.S. Virgin Islands are 100% deductible as a business expense.

This rule is a that you can easily take advantage of by setting up a one-on-one necessary business meeting anywhere in the world outside of the United States and the District of Columbia.

You may not be allowed to take advantage of the seven-day rule when you are traveling outside the United States to a convention, seminar, or similar meeting, because there are special rules that apply for these scenarios.

The second exception to the general rule, is that the general rule does not apply to any travel outside the United States unless that portion of time is at least 25% of the total time traveling.

The IRS Internal Revenue Manual states: "Travel outside of the United States generally must be allocated between business and personal. No allocation is made if foreign travel does not exceed one week, or if less than 25% of the trip is personal, then the travel to and from the business destination is allowed in full."

Having multiple meetings can allow you to take advantage of standby days. For example, if you work on day two and day four, day three would be a standby day. You can deduct lodging and meals for standby days when traveling outside the United States. Timing your working days can allow you to deduct the cost of food and hotel during personal vacation days.

Chapter 18

Turn Your Nondeductible Commute into a Tax-Deductible Trip

Turning your commuting miles into tax-deductible can create a significant tax savings. You can convert your daily trip into thousands of dollars of deductions.

If you are commuting 20 miles one way each way and turn it into business miles, it creates over $5,000 a year in additional tax deductions. This calculation was based on a mileage rate of $.50 per mile but the rate has been higher than that for over 10 years. The actual mileage changes each year.

If you are a sole proprietor, this deduction will save you in both self-employment tax and income tax. The self-employment tax on $5,000 is $707 for most people (depending on profit). If you are in the 22% income tax bracket your total tax savings would be $1,807 a year.

When you have a home office as a principal office, your commute becomes tax deductible business mileage.

According to IRS Section 280A(c) you can claim a home office based on the portion of your home that you use exclusively and regularly for business. The definition of "regular place of business" is a place where you perform work on a regular business. It does not require that you work there every week or on a set schedule.

One of the best ways to beat the other team is by getting the opponent's playbook. And in this case, we are going to take advantage of the IRS Audit Manual's Home-Office Section. This provides everything you need to know to bulletproof your business use of home.

The best scenario for this is when you only have one office, and it is in your home. To build proof for your administrative use, keep a record of what you are doing of what you are doing while working in your office. This can include your time spent keeping books and records, billing and ordering supplies.

Unfortunately, the IRS provides no clear guidance on what it considers regular use. Therefore, you will need to turn to court cases to get a better understanding. In the Green case, the tax court ruled that more than 10 hours was sufficient for regular use.

Next you can bullet-proof exclusive use by having pictures of the office and showing the office has a business look. For example, having business books on the bookshelves can help to provide your office with a business look.

Keep in mind that exclusive means exclusive, the IRS doesn't make exceptions for your principal office. If you happen to be audited you will need to be able to prove your expenses with receipts, canceled checks, and online payments.

Having an office in your home can provide you with a substantial deduction from additional mileage. However, make sure that you understand the rules and meet the requirements.

Chapter 19

Using the Section 179 Depreciation Deduction

The Section 179 deduction is a valuable tool as a tax strategy. It allows a business to deduct an asset's cost in the first year of use rather than spreading it over several years.

Fortunately, the Tax Credit and Jobs Act (TCJA) created additional opportunities for tax deductions by expanding the Section 179 deduction.

If you have a small to medium-sized business, you can take advantage of the Section 179 first-year depreciation deduction to reduce your taxes in the first year your assets are purchased.

One benefit the Section 179 deduction has compared to bonus depreciation is that it can be used for both new and used assets.

The TCJA permanently increased the maximum Section 179 deduction to $1 million. It had previously been $510,000. Additionally, the new Sect 179 now allows the Sect 179 deduction for more property. It now includes purchasing items such as roofs, heating, ventilation, air conditioning, fire protection, alarm systems, and security systems.

For example, suppose you spend $25,000 to replace a

53

roof on one of your business buildings, and you had an undepreciated basis on an old roof of $10,000. (Undepreciated basis is the remainder of the cost that has not yet been depreciated). You can write off $35,000 as a Sect 179 deduction, which is the new roof's cost and the $10,000 retirement of the old roof.

Another advantage of the Sect 179 deduction compared to bonus depreciation is that you can pick and choose your Sect 179 deduction amounts.

As an example, suppose you buy equipment for $60,000. With Sect 179, you can elect to immediately deduct $40,000 or any amount that you choose, including the full $60,000.

The Section 179 deduction provides a valuable benefit in that you have flexibility in choosing the amount to deduct. However, the Section 179 cannot exceed your "aggregate net taxable business income" from all sources calculated before any Section 179 write-off. Essentially this means you can't create a net operating loss (NOL).

The Section 179 deductions do not reduce your Section 199A qualified property for purposes of calculating your 20% QBI tax deduction.

There is a $25,000 limit on Sect 179 deductions for heavy sport utility vehicles (SUVs) with gross weight ratings (GVWRs) between 6,001 and 14,000 pounds. If you have an SUV, you can still beat the $25,000 limit by deducting bonus depreciation. However, you will be required to apply bonus depreciation to all assets in that class placed in service during that year.

The new Section 179 deduction provides you with more ways to take advantage of immediate tax deductions.

Chapter 20

Bundle Deductions for Additional Tax Savings

Itemized deductions are only deductible if you have enough to itemize.

Many people think that since they are benefiting from the big standard deduction and don't care whether they can itemize

The 2018 tax laws increased the standard deduction in 2018 to $12,000 for singles and $24,000 for couples filing jointly. The standard deduction increases each year. However, the increase in the standard is not as beneficial as it may seem.

Without bundling, many people no longer benefit by itemizing their donations, property tax, mortgage interest and medical bills. At one time people owned big houses and made donations and benefited by claiming these deductions.

The standard deduction was increased but the personal exemptions were eliminated. Before the 2018 tax changes, you received an exemption for each person on your return. The exemption in 2017 was $4,050 so a married couple with no dependents had $8,100.

In fact, many people have paid thousands of dollars more

in taxes since 2018 when the tax changes took effect.

Bundling is a strategy which helps you to take advantage of the 2018 tax changes. Bundling involves timing your expenditures, so they are stacked in one year. The following year you would take the standard deduction.

Bundling donations into a single year allows you to fully benefit from your itemized deductions in the years that you take them and take full advantage of the "free" standard deduction amounts in other years.

Taxpayers that have variable income year to year or the flexibility to defer or accelerate income can especially benefit from this strategy.

However, you may only deduct donations up to 60% of your adjusted gross income if you are donating cash, and up to 30% if you are donating securities.

You can use strategies such as:

- Make a large donation in one year instead of two years

- Pay your property tax a year in advance

- Make extra mortgage interest payments

- Plan any elective surgeries and procedures for the year you itemize

- Donor Advised Funds

Donor-advised funds (DAFs) have been around for a long

time, but interest in them has increased because of both the tax benefits and degree of retained control they provide. You can make big contributions of cash, stock or other assets to a DAF in one year and receive a federal income tax deduction for your donation in that year. Then, you can distribute out contributions to your favorite charities over time. Thus, the assets within the DAF can be invested and grow income within the fund tax-free. Thus, you can create a charitable legacy for your family through the DAF. You need to be aware there's no double-dipping. Because you get a federal income tax deduction for your initial contribution, the distributions to charities from the DAF aren't tax-deductible. Only new contributions would be tax-deductible.

It is important to consult with a tax professional when considering using the bundling deductions strategy to gain the most tax benefit year to year.

Chapter 21

Retirement Strategies for Business Owners

There are four options for business owners. You will want to determine which one best meets your retirement needs.

These retirement plans reduce your tax liability by reducing the amount of your taxable income. It is best to consult with a tax professional before selecting your retirement plan to receive the maximum tax benefit.

401(k)

One popular retirement plan for self-employed people is called a solo 401(k). The IRS considers these to be one-participant 401(k)s.

Many people are familiar with these plans because they are similar to the types of 401(k) plans offered by employers. A solo 401(k) is only for sole proprietors who have no other employees. However, there is an exception if you have a spouse who works in the business and qualifies as well.

One of the best benefits of a solo 401(k) plan is that you can contribute as the employer and the employee, which essentially doubles the contribution amount each year.

As is the case with a 401(k), total contributions cannot exceed $19,500 for 2021. The limit goes up to $20,500 in 2022. For people 50 years or older, you can make up to $6,500 in catch-up contributions. The pre-tax benefits are the same as a standard employer-sponsored 401(k).

SEP IRAs

SEP IRAs involve savings that come from the employer only. It is easy to set up and manage. You can contribute up to 25% of your compensation, up to a maximum of $58,000 for 2021 and $61,000 in 2022.

One advantage is that there isn't an annual funding requirement for a SEP IRA. You also have the option to make contributions regularly throughout the year or one lump-sum deposit during the year. This plan is generally best for sole proprietors. However, you can still use a SEP IRA as an employer of multiple employees. In this case, you'll need to contribute to all eligible employees based on their first $290,000 of compensation annually.

SIMPLE IRAs

A SIMPLE IRA is different than a 401(k), but it also falls under the IRA umbrella. It's essentially a mix between an IRA and a 401(k) since it involves matching contributions. You can use A SIMPLE IRA if you are a sole proprietor, but it's even better for small businesses. A SIMPLE IRA has rules similar to a SEP IRA regarding rollovers, distributions, investments, and other details. One disadvantage is that the contribution thresholds are lower than a SEP IRA. For 2021, the limit is $13,500 in 2021 with a $3,000 excess allowed if you're age 50 or older. For 2022, that total goes up to $14,000 with the same excess for age 50 or older. As an employer, you are required to match up to 3% of each employee's contributions or 2% of each employee's salary for contributors and non-contributors.

Keogh Plans

A Keogh plan isn't as popular as an IRA or 401(k) retirement plan for a self-employed individual. Unfortunately, it's more complicated to set up than the other options. However, it provides an added benefit of more potential growth.

Keogh plans are also commonly known as profit-sharing plans.

The maximum contributions to a Keogh plan in 2021 are limited to $58,000 if the plan is a defined contribution plan. The limit goes up to $61,000 in 2022. If you structure it as a defined benefit plan, you can save even more. The cap for defined benefit Keogh plans is set at $230,000 for 2021 and $245,000 in 2022 or 100% of the employee's compensation.

Contributions to a Keogh plan are on a pre-tax basis, like many other retirement plans. However, a Keogh plan is complex to arrange and requires more paperwork than most plans.

You should ultimately base your decision on your specific financial situation.

If you are a sole proprietor and would like a simple way of saving for retirement, a solo 401(k) or SEP IRA would probably be best. These plans are designed more for sole proprietors and are easy to set up and maintain. They also maximize savings.

If you are self-employed and run a small business, it's probably a good idea to use a SIMPLE IRA. You won't need to do as much paperwork to set one up as you would with a Keogh plan, and you'll be able to maximize the retirement savings of your employees, as well as yourself.

A Keogh plan is probably best for people running a small business who want to make sure you and your employees can contribute large sums to retirement every year. However, these are more complicated to set up.

Chapter 22

Defer Revenue and Accelerate Expense

If you have made a profit projection for the year and your taxes are going to be more than you had anticipated, this is a strategy that you may want to consider to reduce your taxes.

If you are using the cash basis for your tax return your revenue for the year is determined by the date you receive it. For businesses using the accrual basis, revenue is determined based on when it is earned. The vast majority of small businesses that are on a cash basis can have the ability to defer revenue. The accounting basis of your business is reported on your tax return. However, if you aren't sure where to find it on the return, contact a tax professional.

If your business is currently using the accrual basis, you can change to the cash basis by filing Form 3115 to change the accounting method with the IRS. However, it would be a good idea to consult with an expert tax professional before making the change.

You will need to quit billing customers and patients near the end of the year. Customers and patients can't pay when they haven't been billed. By accumulating the December bills and sending them in early January, you can avoid paying taxes on one month's income.

Use the IRS Safe Harbor to prepay your expenses. IRS Regulation 1.263(a)-4(f) contains a safe harbor rule that allows cash-basis taxpayers to prepay and deduct qualifying expenditures up to 12 months in advance without challenge by the IRS. Qualifying expenses include rent payments on offices, lease payments on vehicles, and business insurance. Prepaying office rent and lease payments for up to a year can enable you to significantly increase your deductions. Consequently, taking advantage of this rule can have a huge impact on your tax liability.

If the advance amount of rent paid will cause a problem for your landlord, you can mail the advance rent on December 30. By mailing the advance rent on December 30, you get to deduct it in the current year. Your landlord will get what he wants, advance rent in the year he expected it. He won't claim the rental income a year early because he won't receive it until January. It's a good idea to send the advance check by certified mail so that you can prove the date you mailed it to the IRS.

Before using this strategy, you should determine whether prepaying expenses makes sense. It depends on your tax rate this year and in future years, as well as future changes in tax laws that might raise your taxes. If you expect your income to go up substantially next year, you could be better off not prepaying expenses and instead maximize your deductions for next year.

Chapter 23

Year-End Tax Strategies for Stock Owners

Stock strategies that can drastically reduce your taxes from stock sales. Why pay taxes on stock sales at a 40.8% rate when you could lower the rate to 23.8%?

You may be able to have substantial tax savings by making a few easy adjustments.

Knowing these basic tax rules could provide you with major tax savings:

- On short-term capital gains you can pay taxes at a rate of up to 40.8%. This is due to the combination of the top income tax rate of 37% and paying the 3.8% net investment income.

- The maximum tax rate on long-term capital gains is 23.8%. This is the result of the highest long- term capital gain rate being 20% plus and paying the 3.8% net investment income.

- The tax rate you pay on stock dividends ranges from zero to 23.8%, depending on your income level.

- If your personal capital losses exceed your personal gains, the tax laws limit your capital loss to $3,000 but allows you carry forward the losses in excess of

$3,000 to future years.

- You offset long-term gains and losses before offsetting short-term gains and losses.

- It's advantageous to donate appreciated stock to charity.

- Making a donation of stock that would provide a deductible tax loss would wipe out the tax-deductible loss.

Knowing these tax strategies could significantly lower your taxes:

- Try to offset short-term gains at a possible high rate of 40.8% with long-term losses with rates up to 23.8%. This eliminates the high taxes by offsetting them with low-taxed losses.

- Take advantage of long-term losses to create the $3,000 deduction against ordinary income. Use a 23.8%loss to eliminate a 40.8% gain.

- If you are trying to take advantage of a loss by selling stock, avoid the wash-sale loss rule. If you sell stock and buy substantially identical stock within 30 days, you won't get to recognize your loss on that sale.

- If you have lots of capital losses or capital loss carryovers, consider selling stock that would create offsetting capital gains. You don't want to die with large unused loss carryovers.

- If you give money to your parents to help with living expenses or to your children, give them appreciated stock instead if they will be in a lower tax rate than you. If they are in a low tax bracket, they might not pay any taxes on the capital gains at all.

- If you donate stock to charity, give appreciated stock since you will be able to deduct its fair market value.

- Don't donate stock that would provide you with a loss. Sell the stock first to create a loss and then give the proceeds to charity. For example, suppose you bought stock for $12,000, and it's now worth $2,000. If you donate it, you will get a $2,000 tax deduction. But if you sell the stock first and give the $2,000 proceeds you will also be able to claim a $10,000 stock loss.

Chapter 24

The 20% QBI Deduction for Businesses

The Qualified Business Income (QBI) deduction can provide a substantial savings on your taxes. It was created as part of the Tax Cut and Job Act (TCJA) which began in 2018. The 20% QBI deduction is fairly complex. I will explain the basic principles in this chapter. However, the QBI deduction has too much information to try to explain in this book.

I am the author of the book Simplifying the 2018 Tax Changes, and How It Affects You in case you would like to learn more about the QBI deduction.

Qualified business income is generally defined as the net amount of income, gain, deduction, and loss with respect to any qualified trade or business of the taxpayer. Or simply stated, QBI is the profit received from a pass-through business or sole proprietorship during the year.

The 20% business deduction (QBI deduction) is affected by many circumstances and factors, so determining the best tax entity and tax strategy can be very challenging. Business entities that qualify for the 20% business deduction include sole proprietorships and pass-through entities which include partnerships, S-corporation, Limited Liability Companies (LLC), or a trust that owns an interest in a pass-through entity.

The Schedule C, which is used by sole proprietors to report their business income and expenses, is used to determine the amount of QBI. Schedule E is used to determine rental property profit and QBI. However, not all rental activity is Qualified Business Income. Schedule F is used to determine the QBI from farming. Partnership, LLC's and S-corporation owners will receive a Form K-1 which will report information needed for calculating the QBI deduction.

You might have been thinking it's great that businesses are getting a 20% deduction, but not all Qualified Business Income results in the QBI deduction. The QBI deduction is based on the lesser of the QBI or taxable income, so some businesses won't receive as large of a deduction as anticipated, and some won't get any deduction.

For example, suppose you are married and a sole proprietor and your only source of income on your tax return is from your business and your profit is $24,000. Since the standard deduction for a couple who file Married Filing Jointly (MFJ) is greater than $24,000, your taxable income would be zero. Since the QBI deduction is limited to the smaller amount of your QBI or your taxable income, your QBI deduction would be zero.

For example, suppose you are married and a sole proprietor and your only source of income on your tax return is from your business and your profit is $50,000. If the standard deduction for a couple who file Married Filing Jointly (MFJ) is $24,000, this is how your QBI deduction would be calculated:

- Profit $50,000
- Standard Deduction $24,000
- Taxable Income $26,000
- 20% QBI Deduction $5200

In this case the QBI deduction would not be 20% of the business profit since it would be limited to $5,200.

Additionally, the QBI deduction is phased out at certain income levels. The phaseout rules depend on whether the entity is a specified service trade and/or business (SSTB). An SSTB is any trade or business involving the performance of service in the fields of health, law, consulting, athletics, financial services or where the principal asset of the trade is the reputation of one or more of its employees or owners.

C-corporations do not qualify for the 20% business deduction. The TJTC tax law changed the rate of taxation to a flat 21% rate for C-corps. This was a huge tax deduction for large C-corps. Unfortunately, if you have a C- corporation with a profit of $90,000 or less, your taxes will increase because the tax rate on the first $50,000 of profit was 15%. As a result of this change in tax rate, a C-corporation's taxes could increase by as much as $3,000.

Consequently, you may want to consider changing to a different business entity.

Chapter 25

Strategies for Deducting Employee Meals

Due to the financial impact of Covid-19 on restaurants, Congress passed legislation which makes meals a 100% deductible business expense during tax years 2021 and 2022.

Generally, the IRS allows a 50% deduction for providing employee meals.

However, the IRS allows a 100% deduction under certain conditions.

You can take the 100% deduction for your employee's meals when you provide the meals for your convenience and provide them on your business premises.

The "convenience of the employer" test includes the following:

Employees must remain on the premises for emergency calls during lunch. Employees only have a 30-to-45-minute meal period and can't reasonably eat elsewhere.

Employees are restricted to the premises, and they could not otherwise have options of eating within a reasonable meal period when there are no restaurants nearby.

The IRS rules are different if the employer is providing

71

meals to promote morale or goodwill. In this case the meals are not tax-free to the employees.

If the employer meets the "convenience of the employer" test for more than 50% of the employees, all employee meals qualify as deductible by the employer and tax-free for the workers.

If you take your employees to a restaurant for a meeting, the deduction is limited to a 50% deduction. You are not treated as an employee for this type of benefit if your business is a sole proprietorship or an S corporation. However, you would be able to take the 100% deduction for your employee's meals.

Chapter 26

Take Advantage of Tax-Free Benefits

The IRS allows a nice benefit that many business owners may often overlook.

If you are a business owner, you probably know the saying "you have to spend money to make money."

However, one consideration often missing from business purchases is how to pay for your purchases.

Major banks such as Capital One, Chase and American Express have business credit cards which can earn lucrative rewards points that can be used for travel and other business benefits.

Business credit cards can earn three different types of rewards when you make purchases. These rewards options include transferable points, airline/hotel points, or cash-back.

Transferable points are generally the most lucrative type of credit card rewards, and they are more flexible. With this type of card, when you earn transferable points, you have different ways of redeeming them.

The IRS doesn't tax benefits that you receive from making certain business purchases. The treatment of items such as frequent flier miles, hotel points and cash

73

rewards from credit card purchases as tax-free is a great bonus when making your business purchases.

Since the amount spent during the year for fuel, supplies and maintenance are substantial, the benefits that you can receive can be significant.

By choosing the best payment option and using it on as many business purchases as possible, you can increase the amount of your tax-free benefits.

A nice perk is being provided by the IRS for business owners who take advantage of the opportunity.

Since you will need to make purchases for your business, don't lose out on potential rewards. Take advantage of the IRS's generosity of tax-free income.

When using a credit card, it's important to research the different cards so that you will receive the most benefits.

Chapter 27

Cost Segregation

Cost segregation breaks your real estate property into different components. Some of these components can be depreciated much faster than others.

With a cost segregation study, you turn your property into much more than a building. This allows you to depreciate some of the property much sooner which provides you with deductions and tax savings much faster than if they were spread over more years.

Cost segregation allows you to take deductions sooner so that you can invest the money today and compound it over future years. It can create lots of cash that you can immediately invest if you aren't affected by the passive loss rules discussed below.

The Tax Cuts and Jobs Act (TCJA) increased bonus depreciation from 50% to 100%. Additionally, the new law allows bonus depreciation on qualifying used property.

With cost segregation you can take advantage of these new tax laws.

A cost segregation study can give you quick funds by breaking costs into components. With repair regulations, if you replace a component (such as a roof), you assign a value to the old component and write off its undepreciated basis.

Another benefit of doing a cost segregation study is if you have a large increase in profit and you need a big deduction to offset. If you have depreciable real property which is already being depreciated, you could do a cost segregation study and then do a change in the method of accounting by using Form 3115 to take advantage of the study results.

This will create a one-time lump sum deduction, called a Section 481(a) adjustment, during the year you change your method. This allows you to "correct" your depreciation not taken in prior years and take advantage of the deduction this year.

If any of the property was inherited property, it allows you to increase the basis to its fair market value on the date of death of the owner. Consequently, this restarts depreciation and erases recapture from prior depreciation.

If you live in a community property state, property owned by two spouses as community property receives an increase in basis when one of the spouses dies. As a result of the property basis being increased, you can benefit from the cost segregation by accelerating your depreciation deduction which can provide you with cash which can be immediately invested.

You also need to factor any passive loss rules to make sure that you will realize the benefits that you have found from doing the cost segregation study.

Additionally, you will need to factor any additional

ordinary income depreciation recapture taxes that you may pay if you sell the components from the study.

Obviously cost segregation is very complex. It could take many hours of studying to understand all the details.

If you own real estate, you may want to discuss the possibility of cost segregation with your tax professional to see if a cost segregation study could provide you with an immediate source of cash.

Chapter 28

Deduct Your Cell Phone

Deducting business use of your cell phone can provide significant tax savings.

If you use your cell phone for business, you may be able to claim a business deduction. Therefore, it's important to know the IRS rules for deducting cell phone usage so that you are taking the correct amount of business expense.

If you use your own mobile device for business purposes, a cell phone business expense is based on the portion of the time that it is used for business. If 85% of your minutes in a given month are for business calls, for example, you can deduct 85% of your monthly bill on your taxes.

The best way to calculate and document this percentage is by using your cell phone bill, if it itemizes your calls. Many cellular provider bills aren't itemized, but you can log on to the provider's website to access a log of all your calls for the month. Then print out the logs and save them in case you are audited.

You can also try to prove business use through recording daily business logs that show phone conferences, but that's a lot harder. However, if a question ever arises, daily logs may help establish that a call was made for a business purpose.

Some people use two phones, one for business and the other for personal use. If you're strict about keeping them separate, you can normally deduct 100% of the cost of the business phone on your tax return.

If you have one cell phone, it's a big mistake to claim you used it 100% of the time for business. That's a red flag during an IRS audit, since they will assume that even phones that are used primarily for business occasionally are used to make a text or call for personal reasons.

In addition to deducting a percentage of your regular monthly bill, there may be other expenses which you can deduct.

Roaming or other long-distance charges that are required by your business may be deducted. You can also deduct the difference between a more expensive plan needed for business and a cheaper plan that would be sufficient for personal use. Additional services such as call waiting and forwarding that are only used for business are deductible.

Phone apps that you use for business may be deductible. For example, an app that tracks your business mileage would be deductible.

When an employer provides an employee with a cellphone primarily for business reasons, the business and personal use of the cell phone is generally nontaxable to the employee. Therefore, this can be a great benefit for an employee. The IRS does not generally require recordkeeping of business use in order to receive this tax-free treatment.

79

Chapter 29

Tax-Free Fringe Benefit Deduction for Your Smartphone or Tablet

Your type of business entity makes a big difference when it comes to the personal tax benefits from deducting your smartphone or tablet.

And you can even achieve these tax benefits without keeping any tax records on your smartphone usage, depending on your type of entity.

If you have employees or independent contractors, you can pay for their smartphones, and you are not required to keep any phone usage records.

The employees who can benefit from a smartphone include you if you are an employee of your corporation. The benefit includes partners in your partnership, and directors in a corporation. It also includes independent contractors performing services for you. However, it does not include you if you're a sole proprietor.

The employee's or partner's personal use of the smartphone is excluded from income as a de minimis fringe benefit. Consequently, the employee or partner does not have to keep records of business use.

The business can also choose who gets the smartphone

benefits, and this can be only you.

The business must provide this smartphone benefit to the employee or partner primarily for "noncompensatory business purposes". An example of this purpose includes the employer needing to contact the employee at all times in case of an emergency. Another example is if the employer requires that the employee be able to contact clients when they are away from the office. It is also allowed if the employee needs to speak with clients located in other time zones at times outside of the employee's normal workday.

The business is not required to buy the smartphone and its calling plan for the employee or partner. Instead, the business has the option to pay the employee a cash allowance and/or reimburse the actual plan use.

If you own an S corporation, your corporation can reimburse you for the entire monthly fee even though you use the phone for both personal and business calls.

The sole proprietor and the single-member LLC smartphone break would apply to your employees, but not to you if you are a sole proprietor or the owner of a single-member LLC.

If you are a sole proprietor, you are required to provide proof of your percentage of business use. If you use the smartphone 80% for business and 20% for personal, your proprietorship deduction for expensing, depreciation, and monthly charges is based on your 80% business use. In order to prove the 80%, you need to keep track of your calls. An easy method is simply to add the business and personal calls that show on your smartphone bill as proof of your business and personal use.

You won't have to go through every smartphone bill for the entire year and categorize every call. If you make about the same number of calls every month, you can use the sampling method for three months.

If you don't want to calculate the percentage of business calls, you can make it easier by having two phone numbers for your smartphone and use one for business and one for personal use. Current technology now makes this possible.

The biggest advantage for smartphone use is for the partnership or corporation since they can pay or reimburse 100% of your smartphone expenses, even when you use the smartphone for both business and personal purposes. Additionally, the corporation or partnership can pick and choose which employees or partners get the fringe benefit.

Chapter 30

Use a Health Savings Account to Create Tax-Savings

A Health Savings Account (HSA) is a type of savings account that can help you pay for medical expenses, which will also provide the benefit of reducing your taxes.

Fortunately, you can take advantage of the tax savings immediately.

With an HSA you receive money that is tax-free.

One of the best benefits of an HSA is that when you make a contribution, you're getting tax-free money.

Instead of receiving the money immediately when you get paid, the money goes into an HSA for you to spend on medical bills.

Another advantage of an HSA is that your money grows tax-free. An HSA is a health savings account, so it is similar to a savings account and earns interest. But unlike a regular savings account where interest earned will be counted as taxable income, your HSA contributions can grow without the interest being taxable.

There's another benefit of an HSA. When you turn 65, your HSA will become like a traditional IRA. You can withdraw funds from your HSA for anything you'd like, not just qualified medical expenses. Although you will have to pay taxes on those funds when you do. However, you may be in a lower tax bracket when you are retired.

With an HSA, not only are you setting aside money for current medical expenses but you're also able to save for future health care costs. Whether it's this year or 10 years from now, when the time comes to make a withdrawal, you can take that money out tax-free as long as it's for a qualified medical expense.

If you have a high deductible health plan (HDHP), you should consider opening a health savings account (HSA).

Using an HSA is like a savings account that you can use for qualified medical expenses. It can pay for everything from motion sickness medicine to band aids.

There are only 3 requirements for having an HSA.

- You need to be enrolled in an HDHP. That means your health insurance plan has a minimum deductible of $1,400 for single coverage or $2,800 for family in 2021 and 2022. Additionally, it means a maximum annual out-of-pocket expense of $6,900 for individuals and $13,800 for families. This includes medical expenditures like deductibles, coinsurance, and copayments, but not your premium.

- You can't be enrolled in Medicare.

- You must be 18 years or older and no one can claim you as a dependent on their tax return. The

84

maximum annual HSA contribution that you can make as an individual is $3,650. For families, that number goes up to $7,300. If you're 55 and older and not enrolled in Medicare, you can also make an annual "catch-up contribution" of $1,000. These are the limits in 2022.

For example, if you have a family and you contribute $7,300 and are in the 22% tax bracket, you will save $1,606 in taxes.

If you are self-employed, you contribute pretax, and it won't count toward your taxable income.

If you own a corporation, your employer (your corporation) takes money out of your paycheck which reduces your taxable income. However, you still get to use the money to pay medical bills and it's tax-free.

An HSA is easy to set up and a great way to earn tax-free money if you qualify.

Chapter 31

Using the Qualified Opportunity Zone Fund

A qualified opportunity fund is an investment in a designated low-income community, known as a qualified opportunity zone.

The Tax Cuts and Jobs Act (TJAC) tax reform's new qualified opportunity fund provision enables you to permanently defer capital gains.

Qualified opportunity funds create an ability to defer (and potentially eliminate) some capital gains. However, you need to be aware of the requirements and decide if it will be beneficial for you.

Each state's governor chooses which census tracts in their states are qualified opportunity zones. Some designated zones are adjacent to low-income areas that have considerable reclamation nearby which make them valuable for development.

The qualified opportunity fund is required to be a corporation or partnership for federal tax purposes. If a qualified opportunity fund would be beneficial, a sole proprietor should consider changing the entity to a corporation. You could also form a partnership with your spouse, or a friend and you can determine your percentage of ownership of the partnership.

A pass-through entity can choose to use this provision, or only partially defers an eligible gain. If it doesn't use the provision, then you as a partner, shareholder, or beneficiary can elect to use the opportunity zone capital gains tax deferral for the eligible gain that passes through to you. A pass-through organization is an entity other than a sole proprietor or C corporation.

The gain must meet 3 requirements:

- The gain must be a capital gain and can be either short term or long term.

- You would have to recognize the gain for federal income tax purposes before January 1, 2027, without this provision.

- The gain can't be from a sale or exchange with a related person.

After you sell your gain property and recognize the gain, you have 180 days to invest the gain proceeds into the qualified opportunity fund.

The 180-day period starts on the day you would normally recognize the gain for federal income tax purposes.

If your gain is from a pass-through entity, then your 180-day period starts on the last day of the taxable year of that entity.

You are only required to invest the amount of gain you realized on the sale, or the portion of the gain that you want to defer. You keep the basis.

You aren't required to make a one-time investment to obtain a deferral. You have the option to invest the capital gain you want to defer over time in different properties. However, each investment needs to meet the 180-day period for your sale or exchange.

If you decide to defer, you make the election to defer the capital gain on your tax return. The election is on a per-sale basis so if you have multiple sales they will qualify if they meet the requirements.

This strategy is most beneficial when you have appreciation in your qualified opportunity fund, and you hold the investment for at least years so that the appreciation becomes tax-free when you sell it.

Chapter 32

Deduct Self-Employed Health Insurance

If you pay for your own health insurance and you are self-employed, you may be eligible to take this deduction. If you are entitled to deduct it, be sure that you take it because it can be a large deduction.

Self-employed people who qualify are allowed to deduct 100% of their health insurance premiums. This includes dental and long-term care coverage for yourself, your spouse, and your dependents. It is a special personal deduction for the self-employed, however it is not a business deduction. This deduction applies only to your federal, state, and local income taxes, not to your self-employment taxes.

There are two requirements to qualify:

- You can't be eligible for health insurance maintained by your employer or your spouse's employer.

- You can only deduct as much as you earn from your business. If your business doesn't have a profit, you aren't eligible for the deduction.

You can't combine the income from all your business for purposes of the income limit. You can only use the profit from a single business that you designate to be the health insurance plan sponsor.

If you qualify, you can claim the health insurance deduction whether you purchase your health insurance policy as an individual or have your business pay for it. When purchasing your health insurance plan in the name of one of your businesses, that business will be the sponsor. The IRS also allows you to purchase your health coverage in your own name and still get the self-employed health insurance deduction. If you have several businesses, this may be advantageous since it allows you to pick which of your businesses will be the sponsor at the start of each year. Obviously, you would want to pick the business you would think will earn the most money that year.

If you have more than one business, you can have one purchase medical insurance and the other purchase dental insurance and deduct 100% of the premiums for each policy, subject to the income limits discussed above.

Because the self-employed health insurance deduction is a personal deduction, you take this deduction directly on your Form 1040 (it does not go on your Schedule C if you're a sole proprietor). If you itemize your deductions and do not claim 100% of your self-employed health insurance costs on your Form 1040, you may include the rest with all other medical expenses on Schedule A, subject to the 7.5% of Adjusted Gross Income limit (for 2017 through 2020). The limit goes back up to 10% of AGI in 2021. You would have to do this, for example, if your health insurance premiums exceed your business income.

Chapter 33

Take Advantage of the Change in Business Loss Rules

Beginning in 2021, a business can't carry back a net operating loss (NOL) and get an immediate refund of needed cash.

Congress passed the Tax Cuts and Jobs Act (TCJA) which reduced your ability to take advantage of business losses. However, due to Covid-19, Congress retroactively suspended the new rules for tax years 2018 through 2020. This allowed businesses who suffered tax losses to carry back a loss to previous years and get refunds which could immediately help their business.

The Cares Act changed the TCJA limitations for NOLs for tax years 2018 through 2020. The Cares Act allowed carry back the NOL for 5 years and carry it forward indefinitely. Additionally, an NOL could offset up to 100% of your taxable income.

Beginning in 2021, the Cares Act loss rules no longer apply. If you have a business loss, you can no longer carry it back and get an immediate refund. Additionally, an NOL can only be used to offset up to 80% of your taxable income before your 20% Section 199A deduction.

The new NOL rule could have a negative impact on businesses that are struggling financially and in need of immediate cash.

Several strategies make your business loss work for you by immediately offsetting income and providing immediate cash.

Most small businesses use the cash method of accounting for tax purposes. When using the cash method, you recognize taxable income when you receive the cash.

This strategy is to receive the taxable money this year and pay the deductible expenses next year. You can speed up cash received by accelerating your invoices. Offering discounts to clients who prepay for next year's services can entice them to pay early. You can increase your efforts to collect aged receivables and can also consider selling aged receivables to a factoring company.

Another strategy is selling your appreciated property. You can use the business loss to offset the taxable gains. Sales of assets with short-term gains and ordinary income will provide the most tax benefit. You can immediately repurchase similar assets since there is no "wash sale loss" rule.

You can use your business loss to take out IRA funds, and the money will be 100% tax-free. The business loss will offset the taxable IRA distribution.

Another strategy is converting traditional IRA assets to Roth assets regardless of income. You will include the conversion amounts in your taxable income, but you won't pay a 10% penalty on the converted amount. The conversion is tax-free, and your converted funds continue
92

to grow tax-free. An additional benefit is that it will reduce future income from required minimum distributions (RMDs). You are not required to RMDs from a Roth IRA account.

By being proactive, you can bypass the NOL rule and take advantage of the business loss immediately.

Chapter 34

When and How to Use Employees and Sub-Contract Labor

It is important to know the advantages and disadvantages of hiring subcontractors and how it would affect your business. Different projects may require a different hire, so it's best to make the consideration on a case-by-case basis.

Hiring a contractor has many advantages.

Subcontractors require less commitment and responsibility. Hiring employees is an investment of time and money. You will assume the cost of mentoring, training, and managing the employee. If you make a poor choice, it takes time and effort to terminate them and hire a more qualified replacement.

Hiring a subcontractor provides flexibility. You can contract the services you need when you need them. If you don't need their service on a regular basis, it generally makes more sense to hire an independent contractor.

Subcontractors can offer specialized services. Educating an employee to complete a short project could be far more expensive.

Independent contractors can be more affordable. You may pay more per hour for an independent contractor, but your total cost can be less. The cost of payroll taxes, workers comp insurance, unemployment, and health care benefits can be a substantial expense. You don't need to provide office space or pay for computers and other equipment when hiring contractors.

There are several disadvantages of hiring independent contractors.

You have reduced control when hiring a contractor. You can't oversee day-to-day activity or determine how they get the work done. They can work for other clients, so you can't assume they will make your projects their top priority. If it's essential to have significant control over what your workers are doing and how they're doing it, hiring employees is the better option.

Employers often use contractors only for relatively short-term projects.

Consequently, workers are constantly coming and going, which can be inconvenient and disruptive. And the quality of work you get from various contractors may vary.

Employers who want the same quality day after day are better off hiring employees.

When using subcontractors, there isn't as much accountability after the project is complete. Employees will be held responsible long after the project is finished.

For each project, you should consider all the benefits and drawbacks of hiring an employee or contractor.

Then decide on the most important requirements to determine the best option.

If you decide to hire subcontractors, there must be clear communication and cooperation between both parties. You've got to be on the same page about your goals as well as the terms and conditions of your contract.

Include a non-disclosure clause if you will be sharing confidential information.

General liability coverage can get messy in this type of relationship if a client sues and holds you responsible.

It's generally a good idea to have an attorney review any contract before signing it.

It's crucial to know the difference between a subcontractor and an employee for tax purposes. I will be covering this topic in a future column.

Severe consequences for misclassifying workers as contractors

Most businesses are not aware of the extent of the severe penalties for classifying workers as subcontractors when they are considered employees by the IRS and other agencies.

First, failing to properly classify a worker as an independent contractor can result in devastating penalties by the IRS.

Normal employee wages are subject to FICA (Social Security and Medicare) and income tax withholding. If

96

the IRS determines that an individual has been misclassified, it can levy several penalties against the employer in addition to requiring payment of back taxes.

The employer can be responsible for a penalty of up to 3% of the wages, plus up to 40% of the FICA taxes that were not withheld from the employee and up to 100% of the matching FICA taxes the employer should have paid.

If the IRS decides that the employer misclassified its employees intentionally, the penalties are even greater.

In addition to the taxes, the business will also be required to pay a Failure to Pay Taxes penalty equal to 5% of the unpaid tax liability for each month up to 25% of the total tax liability. The IRS will also add interest on the taxes and penalties.

Additionally, a $50 fine can be assessed for each Form W-2 the employer failed to file on such employees.

The longer the employer misclassifies the contractor, the more IRS tax, penalties, and interest will accumulate.

Penalties can be levied by the state for failing to withhold state income taxes if the state requires the taxes to be withheld.

Businesses can be held responsible for failure to pay overtime under the federal Fair Labor Standards Act (FLSA) and applicable state wage laws.

Both criminal penalties and liability for back wages may be levied by employers and executives that violate the FSLA laws.

Businesses can be held liable for failure to comply with federal I-9 requirements. Employers are required to keep properly filled out I-9s for each employee.

Employers can be required to pay penalties for failing to pay the appropriate amount of money to the state unemployment insurance fund.

Businesses can be penalized for violation of state worker's compensation insurance laws for unpaid premiums.

Anti-Discrimination violations under both federal and state law may be assessed for improperly classifying contractors.

Businesses may have liability exposure for failing to provide leave and reinstatement to eligible employees under the Family and Medical Leave Act (FMLA).

Failing to count misclassified workers in determining federal WARN Act compliance obligations in the event of mass layoffs can result in penalties.

As you can see, it's crucial to know the difference between a subcontractor and an employee for tax purposes. I will be covering this topic in a future column.

Strategies to ensure workers are properly classified as contractors

There are many advantages of hiring an independent contractor instead of an employee. The advantages include the reduction in payroll taxes, workers compensation, and benefits. However, the IRS definitions for the difference between a contractor and an employee can be cloudy.

Failure to correctly classify workers can result in substantial penalties from the IRS and other government agencies. Consequently, it's critical to ensure that these government agencies won't disagree with your classification in the event of an audit.

To avoid an independent contractor being reclassified as an employee, it is advantageous to use the following strategies.

Document your business's policy for determining whether a worker is a contractor or employee. This shows that your organization uses guidelines it follows rather than basing the decision on how it provides the most benefit to the company. Your policy should detail the qualifications it uses to determine the proper relationship. It's advantageous to include the guidance on the IRS website to set your policy.

Don't make the mistake of giving your contractor your business cards. It may seem harmless but independent contractors should never represent themselves as part of your organization. If a contractor has its own business cards it helps to prove that it is not part of your company. Their cards should not include your organization's logo or any of your other business information.

Hire independent contractors whose business is structured as an LLC, corporation, or partnership. Hiring a sole proprietor who is structured as an LLC provides an additional factor to help establish that they have their own business.

Avoid paying an independent contractor on a fixed or regular basis. Paying them on a project basis or a percentage of completion basis helps to indicate that they are a contractor. Employees are normally paid an hourly wage or salary.

Having them invoice you for their services will help to establish that they are an independent contractor. Employees may turn in an expense report for reimbursement, but they don't invoice their employer for their services.

Hire independent contractors who work for other businesses. If your contractor works for other companies, it helps to prove they are in business for themselves.

The more businesses your contractor works for the more obvious it becomes that they are not your employee.

Avoid thinking that you won't get caught. If a contractor feels like they are entitled to be treated as an employee, they could turn you in to make you responsible for their payroll tax. Or they could report you if your relationship deteriorates.

If you misclassify a worker, it could be extremely costly since you could be forced to pay huge penalties from the IRS and other government agencies. It's important to know the IRS rules for classifying a worker and use as many strategies as possible to make your case.

Chapter 35

Turn Charitable Contributions into Deductible Business Expense

The Tax Cuts and Jobs Act (TCJA) makes it harder for you to benefit from your contributions.

The TCJA made the standard deduction much larger, however it eliminated personal exemptions which reduced the actual benefit of the larger standard deduction.

The larger standard deduction also made it more difficult for most people to benefit from their donations.

Fortunately, there is a way for you to benefit by deducting it as a business expense.

If you are a business owner, you may be able to make a few modifications and use it as a different type of deduction. This can increase your tax savings from the donation.

A sole proprietor pays income tax and self-employment tax. When you itemize and deduct it as a charitable contribution it only reduces your income tax. Consequently, you have a bigger tax savings when you deduct it as a business expense.

Deducting your donation also reduces your adjusted gross income (AGI). You may receive additional benefits from this because it may enable you to take more non-business credits.

You can convert a charitable contribution into a business expense by changing the contribution to advertising or marketing.

There are several ways that you can take advantage of this strategy.

You may be able to deduct it as advertising.

For example, you could have a fundraiser for your church or another charity. Let everyone know that you are the sponsor and give a short speech about how your services could benefit the people attending.

Another strategy is to give a percentage of the sales proceeds to a charity.

Let your customers know that you will donate a percentage of your sales proceeds to charity. This would encourage your customers to buy your products or services because they know they would be supporting a good cause.

You could use a coupon with one of your products or services.

For example, the coupon could say that the customer should send the coupon to the charity to help the charity.

You could also use a rebate to deduct the business

expense.

The donation must have a direct relationship to your business. Fortunately, you can deduct it even if you have a reasonable expectation that the financial benefit will exceed the amount you paid.

It's important to have a record of the amount spent for the activity, and document because you would expect the expenditure to bring in additional revenue. It's a good idea to have a dollar estimate of your return on investment.

This strategy can be used for business entities other than a sole proprietorship, although it reduces both income tax and self-employment tax for a sole proprietorship.

It's a win-win situation since it can help a charitable organization and reduce your taxes.

Chapter 36

Take Tax Credits for Historic Buildings

Historic buildings can provide a prestigious location for your company and can be beneficial for your business.

If you buy and restore a historical building, you can get a tax credit for the cost of restoration.

State and federal governments are offering tax credits for owners of these buildings. This provides an excellent opportunity for companies to benefit from doing business in a prestigious building.

Tax credits are far better than tax deductions because they give you a dollar-for-dollar reduction in the amount of your taxes. For example, if you spend $100,000 and get a 50% credit, it will reduce your tax liability by $50,000.

Your total tax credit could cover as much as 70% of your rehab depending on what state you live in.

You can find these buildings by going to the National Park Service website (www.cr.nps.gov) and search for historic places.

Then contact your state's historic preservation office to

find additional information. State offices offer valuable information and can provide assistance that will help you during the entire process.

Before proceeding you should find an architect who is experienced in historic preservation. The Secretary of the Interior will need to certify the rehab as bona fide historic rehabilitation.

You will want to make sure you are going to make a profit from this plan. It's a good idea to run the numbers using the after-tax adjusted rate formula (also known as the managed internal rate of return, or MIRR). Many real estate investment programs include this computation. Contact your local Realtor's office for more information.

The federal tax credit has a five-year recapture period that you will need to be aware of before selling the building. This means if you sell the property within 5 years you will have to repay some of the credits. However, after the five-year period is over you will benefit from 100% of the increase in the property's value.

If you are a high-income earner, you should contact an expert tax professional to see if you will be affected by the alternative minimum tax (AMT). You may not be able to take advantage of the credit in the current year if you are paying AMT. However, you can carry the denied credits forward for up to 20 years.

Tax credits can help you to be able to afford the purchase and restoration of an historic building.

Restoring an historic building could provide your company with prestige while giving you and your employees a beautiful place to work. You could also create a substantial gain for your business and restore the charm in your community.

Chapter 37

Filing an Extension

There are several advantages of filing an extension.

It gives self-employed taxpayers an additional six months to put money into their SEP retirement which can provide substantial tax savings.

It can improve the accuracy of your return. With the rush to get tax returns finished by the April deadline, taxpayers and accountants can make mistakes when they are rushing. An extension gives time to make sure everything is complete and accurate.

Extensions can reduce your tax preparation fees. Some accountants raise their fees as the April deadline approaches and lower the fees after April 15. You may be able to save money by filing after the rush.

There is another advantage when filing an extension. I have had clients who thought they had provided all of their income when I prepared their tax return. But unfortunately, they had overlooked sources of income. The missed income is often a 1099-R from their retirement or a missed 1099-MISC when they are self-employed.

Filing an extension gives you enough time to retrieve

107

your wage and income transcripts from the IRS. This ensures that all sources of your income are being reported on your tax return. Normally, wage and income transcripts aren't available from the IRS until after April 15. Your wage and income transcripts can be accessed from the IRS website, or you can have your tax professional retrieve them. Filing an extension provides you with enough time to access your IRS transcripts. An extension may be filed by using Form 4868.

Unfortunately, I have encountered many clients who have had misconceptions about filing an extension.

I have had clients who thought that if you filed an extension, the IRS will be mad, or that they will be more likely to audit you. The IRS doesn't care anymore whether you file an extension than the police care if you take the interstate. In general, everyone is entitled to file for an extension, and the IRS doesn't care. In fact, there was a time when you were less likely to be audited if you filed an extension, but this no longer applies. Filing an extension does not increase your chance of being audited.

There are a couple of exceptions which do not allow you to file an extension. If you previously signed up with the IRS for a special program for paying past due taxes, and have committed to filing by April 15, or if you have filed for bankruptcy, you may need to file by April 15.

I have had many clients who thought if you file an extension and file your return after April 15, that you will have penalties. Filing an extension eliminates the late filing penalty.

The IRS imposes two types of penalties. The late filing penalty is the larger penalty and is 5% of the tax liability for each month it is late and a maximum penalty of 25%. The late payment penalty is only a half of percent a month, which is relatively small. You can make a payment with your extension if you want to avoid this penalty. Any overpayment will be refunded when you file your return.

If you know you have a refund or don't owe taxes, you don't even need to file an extension for your personal income tax return. Any penalties are a percentage of the amount you owe. If you don't owe taxes, there is no penalty, since any percentage of zero is zero. However, I would encourage most people to file an extension in case they are wrong and actually owe the IRS money. Keep in mind that if you file your return more than three years after the deadline the IRS will not give you your refund.

Chapter 38

Interacting with IRS Employees

I can't stress strongly enough the importance of always treating IRS employees with courtesy and respect. This will probably shock many of you, but I actually look forward to talking with IRS employees. I always treat them with courtesy and respect, and 99% of the time, it is a very pleasant experience. Of course, if you start with a different attitude, you may get different results.

If an IRS employee is waiting for my fax or looking up information on the computer, I will normally try to make small talk. I will start by asking them where they are located and how their weather is. I have found that by making small talk and getting to know them, they will often go above and beyond what they are required to do.

Occasionally when I call the IRS, an employee may be having a bad day, but this happens with everyone. If I happen to talk with an IRS employee who seems to be having a bad day, I try to get off as quickly as possible and call again and talk with someone else. An advantage that I have as a licensed legal representative is that I can call the IRS on the Tax Practitioner Hotline and typically I can get through in a few minutes, so calling back is not a big deal. This is one advantage of using a tax pro.

If I happen to disagree with them, I am still as nice and

polite as I can possibly be, and I find that they treat me the same. If you disagree with an IRS employee and are frustrated with your results, tell the employee that you think it may be more effective in resolving the issue if you could talk with their supervisor.

When you talk to an IRS employee on the phone, you should always request certain information and be sure to write it down and keep it where you can easily locate it. Request the following: their name, their badge number, their position and title, address, date and time of conversation, and the information discussed.

When resolving a tax problem, it's important to agree on the next steps and the timeline, which includes deadlines for sending documentation.

Whenever you are mailing documents to the IRS, send them using a method that provides a return receipt.

If you fax documents to the IRS, be sure to print a fax confirmation. I generally staple the confirmation to the document that I have faxed. This makes the confirmation very easy to find.

During an audit, be courteous and avoid being combative, you never want to alienate the auditor. Treating the auditor with courtesy and respect will normally result with them treating you with kindness and respect. This is very important in an audit.

Chapter 39

Using the IRS Playbook

You have a huge advantage when you already have the opponent's playbook.

The Internal Revenue Manual (IRM) is the handbook for IRS employees. It has detailed instructions on how to perform administrative and procedural matters, such as how to audit specific tax returns, collect taxes, process returns, or assess penalties.

The IRM is much easier to read than the tax code since its purpose is to provide instructions for IRS employees.

The IRM could be the most important tool provided to IRS employees since it contains the information to help them do their jobs. Most people are completely unaware of the IRM when they are dealing with their IRS problems. The IRM is not the actual tax law, but it contains the IRS procedures that the IRS employees are supposed to follow. Tax professionals use the IRM to understand what an employee's instructions are for certain situations. When looking for real legal authority, tax professionals turn to the Internal Revenue Code, Treasury Regulations, and court cases.

However, understanding how IRS personnel are supposed to perform certain procedures can provide extremely valuable information. For example, knowing how the IRS will audit deductions on a return (such as the techniques they use or the items they request) can help you to be prepared. If an IRS employee goes rogue by doing something outside of the IRM, you can inform the employee that they are not following the procedures in the IRM and are taking matters into their own hands. Tell the employee what they are instructed to do according to the section of the IRM that you have found. If the employee refuses to follow the IRM, you can request to speak to their manager. This frequently results in a change of attitude when they realize that you know what you are doing.

The IRM has a table of contents so that you can easily find information about the tax matter that you are trying to research. The IRM can be accessed online at irs.gov/irm.

The IRM was made publicly available as a result of the Freedom of Information Act.

In the Internal Revenue Manual, the IRS states:
The IRM is the primary, official source of "instructions to staff" that relate to the administration and operation of the IRS. It details the policies, delegations of authorities, procedures, instructions, and guidelines for daily operations for all IRS organizations. The IRM ensures that employees have the approved policy and guidance they need to carry out their responsibilities in administering the tax laws or other agency obligations.

Using the IRM can be an extremely valuable tool when trying to resolve your IRS problems; however, if your tax issue is complex or involves a substantial amount of money, hiring an expert tax professional may be your best option.

113

Chapter 40

Strategies to Avoid Problems with the IRS

Causes of Audits

If you are like most people, getting an IRS audit letter is something you would like to avoid at all costs. I will cover the most common causes, so hopefully, you will avoid it.

Rounding numbers to zero

Rounding your numbers increases your chances of being audited. I have had many new clients who brought in their previous tax returns. I took one glance and knew they had made up the numbers.

If I can detect made up numbers at a glance, the IRS can easily do it. Their computers are set up to detect when too many numbers end in zeros and fives. If your rent is $1,000 a month, leave it at $12,000 for the year. But if your postage is $98, don't round it to $100.

Not completely filling out your return

The IRS scores all tax returns. The higher your score, the more likely you are to be audited. Not completely filling out your return gives you a score. For example, if you are claiming daycare, complete the day care address and zip code.

114

Having a relatively large number anywhere on your return

Any number that is large compared to what is average is more likely to cause an audit. For example, the average fuel cost is normally about 30%. If you report a fuel cost of 50% on your return, it will draw attention from the IRS, and you are more likely to be audited.

This is true in every part of your return. I have a client who built a large new expensive house. He actually bought the materials so that he could deduct the sales tax. This provided him with a huge deduction. When I prepared his return, I warned him that this would significantly increase his chances of being audited since his sales tax deduction would be higher than the vast majority of other people.

I informed him that he needed to make sure he had proof of the sales tax and his other deductions because he was likely to be audited. He later called me and told me he was being audited. Fortunately, he was just asked to fax his receipts to the IRS, which ended the audit.

If it had been a business expense, the IRS would have been likely to audit every business deduction. For businesses, it helps to break down your expense categories into smaller categories. For instance, if you have a large amount of insurance, break it down into categories for liability insurance, workers comp insurance, health insurance rather than combining it all into one insurance category.

One advantage of using a good tax professional is that
115

they should let you know if they see any large numbers that are likely to trigger an audit. It's best to use a preparer who does a large volume of tax returns each year and who has done them for many years. They will have a better idea of what will draw attention from the IRS since they will have seen enough returns to know what will draw the attention of the IRS.

If your repairs appear high, they are more likely to ask if you have had a rebuilt motor. Rebuilt motors are not considered a repair by the IRS since it will extend the life of the asset. They are required to be taken as depreciation. However, you will still have the option of expensing the rebuilt motor in the first year if you choose.

Reporting the expense as a depreciation deduction has several benefits. First it reduces your chances of being audited since your repairs will not be as high. Second, if you were audited the IRS may require you to depreciate it over a number of years if you don't claim it as a Section 179 deduction on the original return. Additionally, it will normally be beneficial when getting a mortgage. This is because mortgage companies generally allow you to add back depreciation. For example, if your profit was $50,000 and you reported a $5,000 rebuilt motor as depreciation, it would be like having a profit of $55,000 when you refinanced.

The most common cause of an audit is the failure to report all taxable income

Be sure to include every source of income that has been turned into the IRS. I've seen many business owners who came to me to get their taxes done who had received 1099s for their business. I'd say, are you sure that is all
116

the 1099s. And they would say, "It should be." If you have any doubt, the best thing to do is to file an extension and get your IRS Wage & Income transcripts. You will need to file an extension because the data isn't populated in the Wage & Income Transcripts until the beginning of the summer. That way, you know that you have included everything that the IRS has.

I've talked to many people who believe that the IRS will be mad if you file an extension, or you will be more likely to be audited. The IRS doesn't care anymore if you file an extension than the police care if you take the interstate.

In fact, there was a time when you were less likely to be audited if you filed an extension, but this is no longer true. Filing an extension does not increase your chances of being audited.

I think it's a much better idea to file an extension and get it right than get a letter from the IRS asking you to meet with a Revenue Agent.

Large amounts for travel and food will cause an audit

If a business has a large amount of travel expense, it's a good idea to break it down into different categories such as hotel, flights, taxi and uber.

You can't really keep the IRS from detecting your food expense. It is required to be entered on the line for meals since you can only deduct 50% of your cost.

If you are trying to avoid being audited when you are having your taxes done, you may want to consider if you want to include all your meal expenses. If you don't have

117

receipts and documentation for all of your other expenses, you might want to reduce your meal expenses.

Failure to file your returns on time increases your chances of being audited

I've had new clients who didn't file their return on time because they didn't have the money to pay their taxes.

First, you can get hit with big penalties. The late filing penalty is 5% a month and a total of 25%. So, for example, if you owed $4,000, you would increase your taxes by another $1,000 for not filing on time. And you would be increasing your chances of being audited.

Don't ever make the mistake of not filing because you don't have the money to pay the taxes.

Having previous tax issues will increase your chances of being audited.

Keep this in mind when you are filing your taxes. Those big numbers are likely to get even more scrutiny.

An angry ex-spouse, business associate, family member, or friend can turn you in.

I have seen this happen before. And when they have knowledge about you, the IRS knows exactly what to audit.

Businesses with too many losses

Businesses with too many losses will draw attention from the IRS computers since this can easily be monitored.

Depending on the type of business, the IRS may try to rule that the business is a hobby and disallow previous losses and future losses. If the IRS rules it as a hobby business, you are required to report your income. But with the 2018 tax changes, hobby expenses are no longer deductible. In previous years they were deductible as a hobby expense on Schedule A.

Claiming hobbies as businesses

Lots of people will have horse farms or become fishing guides in order to reduce their taxes. Losses from farming and horse farms, in particular, have been known to draw interest from Revenue Agents.

Not reporting cash sales

A business that doesn't report cash sales when other businesses in the industry do is likely to be audited. As an example, I know of a local computer repair shop that only reported his credit card and 1099 income since that was all that was being turned into the IRS. Other computer repair shops also get paid by cash and check. The IRS noticed that this computer repair shop reported no cash sales. If it goes criminal and you are prosecuted for income tax evasion, I guarantee you will wish you had reported the income.

Claiming large donations

Claiming large charitable deductions relative to your income may draw attention from the IRS. The IRS also checks for appraisals on highly valuable noncash items. Gifts of land easements are also closely scrutinized by the IRS.

119

Deducting Alimony

With the 2018 tax changes, claiming alimony is more complex. The IRS realizes that there will be people trying to deduct alimony who aren't eligible to deduct it. The IRS will be scrutinizing alimony deductions to make sure taxpayers qualify for the deduction.

Business use of the home

Business use of the home is supposed to increase your chance of being audited. However, I have never noticed an increase in audits due to claiming business use of home. I have filed many tax returns each year with the business use of home and have never noticed one audited because of it.

Math errors

If you are preparing your own return without using software, be careful that your math is correct. You should also check to make sure everything has been entered on the correct line.

Claiming the earned income credit

This is because many people fraudulently make up numbers to get a large amount of earned income credit in order to get a large refund. It's ok to take the earned income credit if you are entitled to it. However, be careful when filing your return because you will have an increased chance of being audited.

Having very little income

If your only source of income is your business and you show very little income, you are more likely to be audited. The IRS realizes that people need money to pay for their living expenses. The IRS can question you about how you are paying for your living expenses.

Your mortgage interest is usually reported to the IRS which can cause an audit if your business income is too low. For example, if your mortgage interest is $10,000 and your profit is $16,000 the IRS may ask how you can have a profit of $16,000 and be paying $10,000 in mortgage interest and pay for your property tax, homeowners' insurance, utilities, food and clothing.

Claiming too many business miles

The IRS will compare your amount of business miles to other people's business mileage in the same industry. And deducting a high percentage of miles can cause an audit. This is especially a concern when you claim too high of a percentage and don't have another vehicle available for personal use. For instance, if you claim that all your mileage was for business the IRS is going to want to know how that is possible.

Having assets or cash in another country

The IRS is very interested in taxpayers who have assets and cash stashed in other countries, especially in countries with more favorable tax laws than those in the U.S. The IRS has increased its rules for overseas assets as well as its scrutiny of these tax returns.

The IRS can normally access your account information from a foreign bank. It will do so if it believes that you might owe taxes on the money you've placed there. Some foreign banks are required to provide the IRS with lists of American account holders.

Large cash deposits

As a result of the Bank Secrecy Act, various types of businesses are required to inform the IRS and other federal agencies whenever anyone engages in large cash transactions that involve more than $10,000. The purpose of the Bank Secrecy Act is to reduce illegal activities.

Consequently, you can expect the IRS to question where that money came from if you plunk down or deposit a lot of cash for some reason, particularly if your reported income doesn't support it.

The IRS will be notified if you make a large deposit over this amount. You should be prepared to show how and why you received that money if you file a tax return.

Using unscrupulous and fraudulent tax preparers

Some preparers will do anything they can to get you a large refund. They have even been known to e-file one return with the IRS and give their client a different copy of the return that was filed with the IRS. And they may try to charge you a percentage of your refund. This is illegal.

Some of them tell their clients that they don't need to include the tax preparer information. Be cautious of anyone who prepares tax part-time or doesn't have the

122

necessary education and experience.

When the IRS finds an unscrupulous tax preparer, they normally get a list of all their clients and go through all the returns and find other people to audit.

It's also a good idea to find a preparer who will show you an answer in black and white from an IRS source when you ask them a tax question.

Chapter 41

Strategies for Getting Out of IRS Penalties

First-time abatement

IRS penalties can be steep for filing late. However, if you have been hit with penalties, there may be ways to get out of paying them.

For your partnership or S corporation return, the penalty is $200 per partner or shareholder per month, up to a maximum of 12 months. Additionally, the late payment penalty is 0.5% of the tax owed on the return for each month the tax is unpaid, up to a maximum of 25% of the total tax owed. As an example, if your partnership or S corporation was filed a day late and you have 10 partners or stockholders the penalty is $2,000. That's a huge penalty for being a day late. If it gets lost by the post office or IRS and you are notified by a year or more later, it would be a
$24,000 late filing penalty.

For an individual or C corporation return, the penalty is generally 5% of the total tax owed on the return for each month the return is unfiled, up to a maximum penalty of 25% of the total tax owed.

It's a good idea to have proof of mailing in the event it gets lost. If the post office or the IRS lost your tax return
124

and you don't have proof it was mailed, you may still be able to avoid paying the penalties.

The IRS provides first-time abatement of penalties.

You will qualify if:

- You didn't previously have to file a return, or you have no penalties for the 3 tax years prior to the tax year in which you received a penalty.

- You filed all currently required returns or filed an extension of time to file.

- You have paid, or arranged to pay, any tax due.

The failure-to-pay penalty will continue to accrue, until the tax is paid in full. It may be to your advantage to wait until you fully pay the tax due prior to requesting the first-time penalty abatement.

First-time abatement is the easiest way to get a penalty removed since there is no explanation required for the IRS first-time abatement. It can be used for any reason.

Partnership relief

There is a little-known loophole for late filed partnership returns. If the partnership has 10 or fewer partners and all partners reported their shares of their partnership tax items on their timely filed returns. Additionally, to qualify, you and your partners must be individuals or estates, and you are required to allocate all partnership items according to the partnership interest.

When you call the IRS, ask for relief under Revenue Procedure 84-35.

Reasonable cause

Reasonable cause is not as easy since it requires a legitimate explanation for filing late.

The IRS lists a few situations that may qualify for reasonable cause. You will need to provide specific details.

Examples are:

Death or serious illness which can include you or your immediate family members. You will be required to provide the IRS with detailed information. This includes your relationship to them, the date of death or illness, how the situation prevented you from meeting your tax requirements, how the death or illness impacted your life negatively, and whether you promptly resolved your tax matters once a reasonable amount of time passed.

Fire, casualty, natural disaster, or other disturbance. It's important to let the IRS know if you were in an officially declared disaster area, although it's not a requirement. You will be required to describe the timing of the event, the effect on your personal life or business, and how you attempted to comply as soon as possible.

Inability to obtain records. You will be required to explain why the records were important, why they were unavailable, what steps you took to acquire the records, why you weren't able to estimate, and whether you promptly filed the return and paid the tax once you
126

secured the records. Any documentation that you can provide that shows your efforts in obtaining the information will be helpful.

You should avoid saying things like "I forgot" or "I didn't know the tax laws." The Supreme Court has ruled that you can't blame it on your late filing or payments on your tax preparer, since you are responsible.

Don't give up if the IRS initially denies your request. When the IRS denies your request for penalty relief it is required to send you the denial in writing. The letter will explain how you can dispute the decision with the Appeals Office.

However, you may want to have an expert tax professional represent you.

If you have already paid the penalty, you can still get your money back by using IRS Form 843. However, the deadline is three years from the date you filed the return or two years from the date you paid the penalty.

Chapter 42

Settle IRS debt for less

You have two options that can help you pay a fraction of your tax liability. Options the IRS allows include the Partial Payment Installment Agreement and Offer in Compromise.

The Partial Payment Installment Agreement is an installment agreement that allows you to pay less than the total liability due to the statute of limitations expiring before the entire liability has been paid. In this case, it may be beneficial to use a tax resolution specialist for strategies that can be used to reduce your monthly payment. By reducing your monthly payment amount, you will be able to pay less of your tax liability before the statute of limitations expires.

The Offer in Compromise (OIC) is a contract with the IRS that allows you to settle your taxes for less than the full amount of the liability. An OIC can result in the IRS accepting a small percentage of what you actually owe in taxes. However, the amount that the IRS will settle for depends on your assets and the amount of money you have left after paying your bills each month.

For people who have accumulated a large amount of tax debt, an Offer in Compromise (OIC) may be the best option. An OIC is a method where the IRS settles for a portion of the amount owed. There are several strategies you can possibly use to reduce your OIC. You need to consult a tax professional in order to implement the correct strategy, otherwise you could be wasting money.

These strategies for reducing the amount of your OIC include purchasing:

- business assets
- personal vehicles
- health insurance
- life insurance
- home repairs
- medical/dental procedures

In addition, you can pay for medical bills and living expenses.

Additionally, the amount that you pay your tax professional can be used to reduce the amount of your OIC. Essentially, the IRS is allowing you to pay for your tax professional to reduce your offer amount instead of giving the money to the IRS.

You may be able to get an OIC accepted by the IRS. However, a well-trained tax resolution specialist knows strategies to reduce the amount of an OIC that most taxpayers don't know. These strategies could save substantial amounts of money.

I generally do not recommend that taxpayers file their own OIC because it could cost them as much as tens of thousands of dollars due to an increased amount of the OIC offer. Unless you can get your OIC down to a minimal amount, I would recommend hiring a professional. Additionally, only a small percentage of self-prepared Offer in Compromises are accepted. Many taxpayers fail to realize that the IRS won't accept an OIC if there is another collection method that will enable them to get more money.

Chapter 43

Option if You Can't Pay the IRS

If you don't have money to pay your tax debt, this strategy may work for you.

The Currently Not Collectible (CNC) program suspends IRS collection activity until you have the ability to pay your taxes.

If you have assets with very little cash equity and no income beyond what is needed to live, the IRS may determine your tax liability is currently not collectible. While applying for CNC status, the IRS may ask you to file any past due returns. The IRS employee who is assigned to your case will temporarily remove your case from active inventory. Consequently, this will stop the IRS collection process and stop collection calls, wage garnishment, and bank levies.

Your case will remain in the CNC status until the IRS receives information that your financial situation has improved. CNC status will give you more time to pay off your debt. You should take into consideration that penalties and interest will accrue on your tax liability.

It is important you take action before the IRS starts wage garnishment, bank levies or federal tax liens. If the IRS files a tax lien, you could potentially lose your job.

Generally, ignoring the issue will only make matters worse.

With the CNC Status, you will be required to make payments if the IRS discovers that your financial status has improved. Typically, the IRS requests new financial information about every two years. The IRS may keep your future tax refunds and apply them to your debt. The advantage of an Offer in Compromise is that your tax liability will be permanently eliminated even if your financial situation improves.

Occasionally, the IRS fails to reexamine taxpayers' status. Generally, the IRS has 10 years to collect the debt. This is called the statute of limitations. The statute of limitations starts at the time the tax return is filed. For example, if you file your 2017 tax return in 2021, the statute of limitations would expire in 2031. Usually, if the IRS fails to collect within the statute of limitations, the tax debt will expire.

You need to consult a tax professional to determine if this strategy will work for you. An expert tax resolution specialist may have CNC strategies to make this option successful.

Chapter 44

Dealing with Audits

Know what the IRS is seeking.

Each audit is different, but they are generally trying to determine three things.

1   Did you report all your income?

2   Are your receipts and deductions legitimate?

3   Is your business a hobby?

An auditor will generally examine bank statements to look for unreported income. You should compare your bank statements to the income that you reported before the audit. This will provide you with an opportunity to be able to explain the discrepancy. If there is a discrepancy discovered during the audit and you don't have an answer, it will make a bad impression with the auditor. When an auditor finds unexplained discrepancies, the auditor is likely to scrutinize your documentation more closely during the audit.

Having receipts doesn't necessarily make them a legitimate deduction. The auditor will want to determine whether the receipt was used for business purposes rather than for personal benefit. The auditor will also be trying to determine if the expenditure was normal for your type of business. For instance, if you build a swimming pool at your home for your customers and associates to use, the auditor will question whether this is normal for your type of business.

Many people try to use their hobbies as a tax write off to reduce their tax liability. The IRS is well aware of this and will try to prove your "business" is a hobby if you are showing losses too often. In this case your receipts are real, but the IRS will not consider it a legitimate deduction.

Be completely prepared for the audit

You need to make sure that you have all of the documents requested for the audit and that you have done all necessary research to make your case.

Providing documents

Don't give your original documents or your only copy to the IRS. If the IRS loses your documents, you will have nothing to support your case. IRS auditors have been known to misplace or lose taxpayer's documents. It happens. It is your responsibility to maintain your records.

Don't provide more documentation than is requested. Providing more documentation than is requested only provides the auditor more information to scrutinize for possible audit issues.

Organize your documents

If your records are not organized, the auditor is likely to

think that you have not done a good job of keeping up with your records. The auditor is more likely to go into the audit thinking that you have good documentation for all your expenses if you are organized and may not examine as thoroughly as if your records were sloppy. It may also result in limiting the scope of the audit.

Interacting with the auditor

Treat the auditor with respect and don't be combative. You don't want to alienate the auditor. Try to answer the questions as briefly as possible. Don't talk about anything other than the question the auditor has asked. People are often nervous during an audit and have a tendency to talk too much. People are often aware that what they are saying is self-incriminating and will lead to the auditor wanting to examine more information.

Do not lie to the auditor

Telling a lie to an auditor is a federal crime. Auditors will often ask questions to which they already have the answer, just to see if you are being honest with them. Once you have told a lie you are done. Auditors are not likely to accept your word for whatever you say. If you make a false claim, you will be required to provide false documentation as proof. This can lead to criminal tax fraud or a tax evasion charge. Don't go down that road, you don't want to do anything which could make matters worse.

Try to take charge of the audit

Have every item that is fully documented in front of your organizer. If the auditor asks for documentation which cannot be fully documented, tell the auditor that you have everything already organized and you think it will result in the audit going smoother. When the auditor starts the audit by seeing that those items are documented, he is more likely to be lenient on later items. Auditors generally have four hours to finish the audit. Take your time on the early items that are fully documented during the audit. The auditor may run out of time before getting to the items which are not fully documented.

Disagreements with the auditor

If you disagree with the auditor, don't wait until appeals to disagree. If you feel the auditor is not sticking to the guidelines, you should ask for a managerial conference. You want to use all your possible options to get a different opinion. If the group manager doesn't agree with you, then you can appeal. By doing this, it gives you one more opportunity to receive a different opinion. Tell the revenue agent and manager that you may need to appeal if you can't come to an agreement.

Appeals

If you don't like the results from the audit, you have the right to an Appeal. It is important not to sign any IRS documents that state that you agree with the audit before filing an Appeal. If the audit involves a gray area, you may be successful by taking it to Appeals. However, it would probably be in your best interest to seek the advice of a licensed tax professional if you decide to take your case to Appeals. An appeal requires that you have exhausted all the administrative remedies. You will need to document your discussion with the group manager before going to appeals. Appeals and tax courts will take
136

notice of whether you have exhausted all your administrative remedies.

Avoid going to the audit with your legal representative

In general, if you have legal representation for an audit, you should not attend. If you go to an audit with the legal representative, the IRS can ask you questions. Anything you say can be held against you. I have found that clients tend to talk too much due to being nervous.

Ask if the case is going criminal

If you are in an audit and you are concerned about the types of questions the auditor is asking, you should ask the examiner why he is asking this question. If the revenue agent (RA) is no longer working on your case, it could be because it is being transferred to the criminal unit. There can also be a parallel audit which includes a civil audit and a criminal audit. You can ask if this case is being elevated to another unit, and they are required to tell you. If it is, tell the auditor you wish to stop the audit in order to get legal representation.

Extending the statute of limitations

If you have provided all the requested documentation and the IRS asks you to voluntarily extend the audit, this generally means that the IRS isn't completely prepared. Normally you don't want to voluntarily extend the statute of limitations on the audit, that is the IRS's problem.

Ask for the auditor's work papers

If you disagree with the auditor's findings, after he is
137

finished working on the case, you should request the audit's work papers. You want to see what the auditor has written in the audit report about the audit and you. Under federal law, according to IRC 6103(e), you are entitled to the work papers, but only if you request them. You should review the auditor's work papers before submitting an official appeal. It is best to make a FOIA (Freedom of Information Act) request for the work papers. You can ask the auditor for the work papers, but he can say he will do it when he has time to get to it. With a FOIA they have 20 business days to provide it to you.

You are not required to be at a field audit at your business

According to IRC 6103(c), if the IRS makes a field visit and you have legal representation, you are not required to be there. The representative can represent the taxpayer in any interview.

Auditor requirement of QuickBooks

If the IRS requires your QuickBooks records, give them a printout for only the year requested. Try to avoid giving them access to your QuickBooks software. You should never give them records for any year except what is requested. If the IRS demands your electronic records, close out the other years which are not being requested. Never provide them with the administrative password, they could look at other years or make changes. You can give them a password, but not the administrative password.

Use an audit log

Use an audit log to document all questions you were asked, your answers, and all documentation that you provided. Your records should be well organized, and you should be able to explain the difference between the tax return and the total expenses from your records if they are different.

Your tax preparer should not represent you

Generally, your tax preparer should not represent you in an audit. The IRS considers this to be a conflict of interest. You should use a different licensed representative for the audit.

Recording the audit

If the IRS agent initially comes across as being intimidating, you may want to request to have the audit recorded. This is your right; however, you must make the request at least ten days before the audit.

The IRM

Take advantage of the IRM which is the IRS manual for employees. See Chapter 37 Strategy of using the IRS playbook.

Delaying the audit

Avoid unduly delaying the audit. The IRS normally establishes a date for the audit. If you feel that you wouldn't be ready by that date, ask for more time. You can tell them you need more time to obtain documentation or to review the issues. However, do not keep changing the date of the audit.

139

Ask for legal representation if you don't like where the audit is going

If you don't like where the audit is going, tell them you would like to get legal representation. That will stop the audit immediately. Don't say another word. Pack up your stuff and go home. Get a legal representative as soon as possible.

Chapter 45

Sole Proprietor – Advantages and Disadvantages

This column provides an overview. It is important to research and have a thorough knowledge of all issues or contact an expert tax professional.

A sole proprietor is the easiest and least expensive way to start a business, and it allows you complete control of your business. You're automatically considered to be a sole proprietorship if you do business activities but don't register as any other kind of business.

A small business owner will often choose to start with a proprietorship, and as it grows, change to a different entity.

You can be held personally liable for the debts and obligations of the business.

It can also be hard to raise money because you can't sell stock, and banks are hesitant to lend to sole proprietorships.

Sole proprietorships can be a good option for low-risk businesses who want to test their business idea before forming a more formal business.

When you are an employee, your employer is required to

pay half of your Social Security and Medicare taxes, and the other half is deducted from your paycheck. But when you are self-employed, you must pay all your Social Security and Medicare taxes yourself. This is what is known as the self-employment tax.

Normally, you don't need an employer ID number unless you have employees. If you operate under a different name, you may be required to register a DBA (Doing Business As).

Advantages:

Easiest to start. If you decided the business is going to be successful, you could change to a different entity at a later date.

You have complete control over the decision making for the business.

Avoid double taxation.

Eligible for the 20% QBI deduction.

If you meet the requirements, you can have a deduction for business use of your home. This can be a huge benefit since you can reduce your taxes without incurring any additional expense.

You can deduct your health insurance if you are self-employed.

You can deduct education to become an expert and write off the expense.

Disadvantages:

Self-employment taxes.

Lack of protection against lawsuits. It's a good idea to have liability insurance.

Having another business associate could provide capital and expertise in an area that you lack knowledge of.

Less opportunity for additional funding.

If you become ill or physically impaired, it may be harder to continue your business operations.

Chapter 46

Limited Liability Corporations (LLCs) – Advantages and Disadvantages

Limited Liability Companies (LLCs) are popular for small businesses because of the legal and tax advantages.

An LLC can offer legal protection to its members like a corporation.

Single-member LLCs

LLC owners are called members. Single-member LLCs have only one owner. However, spouses in community property states can elect treatment as a single-member LLC for income tax purposes.

An advantage of operating as a single-member LLC is that it has the benefits of a sole proprietorship while also providing legal benefits. Filing a single-member federal income tax return is very simple.

Single-member LLC businesses that individuals own are reported on a Schedule C like a sole proprietorship. If a single-member LLC is a farming activity, you would report it on a Schedule F. If a single-member LLC is a rental activity, you would report it on a Schedule E of your Form 1040.

144

An LLC also provides liability protection a sole proprietorship doesn't have. However, you may want to consider adding an insurance policy. An LLC does not protect you from liability exposure related to professional malpractice or your tortious acts. Tortious acts are wrongful actions other than a breach of contract, such as negligence when driving a vehicle. It's best to get advice from a business attorney.

Multi-member LLCs

A multi-member LLC is typically treated as a partnership for federal income tax purposes and filed on a partnership Form 1065 return. However, you can elect to treat the LLC as a corporation, but the default is a partnership.

Partnership taxation rules provide more flexibility to make tax-free transfers of assets (including cash) between you and the LLC than an S or C corporation.

A benefit of the partnership rules is that it allows LLCs to make special allocations of taxable income, losses, and deductions among members. The special allocations are beneficial because they can be disproportionate. For example, a 25% member in a high-income tax bracket could be allocated 90% of the LLC's depreciation deduction. The high-income tax bracket member could be allocated more of the LLC's income and gains to compensate for the special allocation of the depreciation deduction taken earlier.

An LLC member can benefit from the 20% QBI deduction on all member income except guaranteed payments.

There are several disadvantages to LLC partnerships.

A disadvantage of the LLC partnership is that partners can be required to pay more self-employment tax compared to an S corporation.

C corporations can provide many more tax-free fringe benefits than LLC partnerships. For example, if the entity is a C corporation, the corporation can deduct the cost of health insurance to the employee shareholders. When an LLC partnership pays health insurance for the members, the payments are reported as guaranteed payment income. Usually, the health insurance can be deducted as self-employed health insurance, but it is still just a wash with no tax benefit.

Don't overlook the consequences of your state taxes. Each state has its own tax laws. State laws may affect your decision-making regarding creating an LLC as your business entity.

Chapter 47

Partnerships – Advantages and Disadvantages

When you decide to start a partnership, everything is new and exciting. You and your friend(s) or acquaintances have a great idea that you envision will grow and be very successful. You may rush to get it up and running as soon as possible, and you may skip some essential steps.

Everyone involved thinks there won't be a need for a written agreement for the future.

In the early days of the business, the owners get along with each other and assume that, whatever happens, they'll be able to work things out. But it's a mistake to think that things will always be that way. Businesses evolve, and so do their owners' goals, visions, and relationships with one another. Eventually, there will be conflict and, without an agreement between the owners, that conflict can be very expensive and emotionally draining.

A better practice is to set up a business legal structure at the beginning that includes an agreement among the owners. The agreement can include such things as how conflicts will be resolved, how to deal with a departing owner, how to take on new owners, and how profits and losses will be divided.

Depending on the type of business entity, you might have a partnership agreement, an operating agreement, or a buy-sell agreement. It costs some time and money upfront to prepare the agreement, but it's far better and cheaper to agree at the outset than to try to resolve an emotionally charged conflict later.

For the above reasons and more, having a good business structure is an important part of any new venture. Before forming a business entity, evaluate the tax implications, choose the right state for formation, sign an agreement with your business partners, and get adequate insurance. Then your business will be on the right path for success.

A limited liability company is a chameleon. It is automatically taxed in the same way as a sole proprietor (if there is one owner) or a partnership (if there are multiple owners). But an LLC also can choose to be taxed as a C corporation or an S corporation. Sometimes, corporate tax status allows an LLC's owners to minimize self-employment taxes or to deduct expenses that would not otherwise be deductible.

Chapter 48

C Corporations – Advantages and Disadvantages

The C corporation (C Corp) is taxed differently than an S corporation (S Corp) or an LLC.

The individual owners of an S corporation or an LLC are responsible for paying their percentage of the business's taxes. The C Corp is responsible for paying the corporate income tax liability rather than the owners. However, the stockholders pay taxes when they report the dividends on their individual income tax return. For example, if you owned stock in General Motors, the corporation would be responsible for paying the corporate income tax liability.

Since the owners of a C Corp are responsible for paying the taxes on their dividends, this can result in double taxation. Dividends may be taxable depending on the amount of the stockholder's taxable income.

The tax rate on qualified dividends is zero for people with lower incomes. A qualified dividend is a dividend that is taxed under capital gains tax rates that are lower than the regular income tax rates on ordinary dividends.

The 2018 Tax Cuts and Jobs Act reduced the highest corporate tax rate from 35% to 21%. Consequently, this change may impact which is the best entity for you.

Sole Proprietors and owners of S Corps and LLC partners are eligible for the 20% Qualified Business Income (QBI) deduction. C corporations are not eligible for the QBI deduction since their maximum tax rate was reduced from 35% to 21%.

Since the 2018 Tax Cuts and Jobs Act had a major impact on the taxes, you could be losing out on thousands of dollars in tax savings if you haven't done a tax strategy analysis since the tax changes.

State taxes must be taken into consideration when choosing the best tax-saving strategy.

When choosing a business entity, it is essential to also consider factors other than taxes.

The C corporation (C Corp) can provide advantages that an S corporation (S Corp) or an LLC cannot.

If you need to raise capital for your business, a C Corp could be your best option. Having unlimited shareholders and multiple classes of stock are advantages that make it more appealing for attracting venture capital and other types of equity financing.

An S corp is limited to 100 shareholders and one class of stock, but a C Corp can have an unlimited number of owners and multiple classes of stock.

A C Corp shareholder can freely sell shares, and the buyer will become the shareholder with all those rights. A member in an LLC is able to sell his or her economic

150

rights but not the management rights. Unless the operating agreement permits otherwise, the LLC member is required to obtain consent from other members to sell the whole interest and have the buyer become a member.

The C corporation also has the advantage of being able to offer stock options.

All corporations are considered to be a C corporation until Form 2553 is submitted to the IRS, which is the election to become an S corporation.

Chapter 49

S Corporations – Advantages and Disadvantages

S corporations can be used for a one-owner business or a business with up to 100 owners. The S corporation has significant advantages but has some tax law restrictions.

Advantages:

Liability protection. Your personal assets are generally protected from exposure to business liabilities under state law. However, no type of entity will protect your personal assets from exposure to liabilities related to your own professional malpractice or your own tortious acts.

Pass-through taxation. Your share of the business's taxable income items, deductions, and credits are passed through to your personal return. There generally is no corporate-level federal income tax, so there is no double taxation that can potentially impact a C corporation.

Opportunity to minimize Social Security and Medicare taxes. This can be achieved by having the corporation pay you a modest but reasonable salary. Your share of the S corporation's remaining taxable income is not subject to Social Security and Medicare taxes.

If you are starting a new business and it is not profitable, the losses will decrease taxable income on the corporation owner's personal returns. If a C corporation has a loss the owners will not be able to take advantage of the loss on their personal returns.

You can convert to a C Corporation at a later date after you have taken advantage of flow-through losses.

Interests in an S corporation can be freely transferred without causing adverse tax consequences.

S corporations usually don't have to use the accrual method unless they have inventory.

Disadvantages:

Salaries received from an S corporation do not qualify for the new Qualified Business Income deduction. In general, all of the profit from sole proprietorships qualifies for the QBI deduction, and partnership income (excluding partner guaranteed payments) also qualify for the QBI deduction.

However, even though it is Qualified Business Income, it may not be eligible for the deduction. The details of the QBI deduction are complex and beyond the scope of this article. I would recommend that you discuss your particular situation with a tax expert to see which entity would provide the most tax savings.

Tax law restrictions. S corporations are subject to several tax law restrictions that don't apply to other businesses. S corporations can have only one share of stock. Non-resident alien individuals are not allowed to be

153

shareholders. An S corporation cannot have more than 100 shareholders and the Owners and employees holding 2% or more of the company's shares cannot receive tax-free benefits.

Shareholders can be individuals, estates, and certain types of trusts.

At the shareholder level, shares are subject to seizure and sale in court proceedings.

Chapter 50

Create an S Corporation to Save Thousands

If you own a business as a sole proprietor, you may be able to save thousands of dollars every year in FICA taxes (Social Security and Medicare taxes).

A sole proprietor pays FICA taxes on the entire profit.

An S corporation has less FICA taxes because it only pays FICA taxes on the salary of its owners, and not the remaining profits which are paid out as dividend distributions.

If you change your business to an S-corporation, you can classify some of your income as salary and some as a distribution. You'll still be liable for FICA taxes on the salary portion of your income, but you'll just pay ordinary income tax on the distribution portion.

For example, if you are self-employed and have a profit of $100,000, your FICA tax would be $15,300.

If your business was an S-corporation and you had a salary of $50,000, the remaining $50,000 would be treated as a distribution that would not be subject to self-employment taxes. This would reduce your FICA taxes by $7,650 ($50,000 x 15.3%).

An S corporation officer with a salary of $50,000 and a distribution of $90,000 would save $13,770.

The IRS requires S corporations to pay their owners reasonable compensation for the service they render to the business. This prevents the owners from paying an unreasonably low amount of FICA taxes or completely avoiding them by having a salary of $0.

The range of a reasonable salary can be a gray area. However, pushing the envelope too far can create the risk for an audit. The IRS has factors to determine a reasonable salary and they include training and experience, duties and responsibilities, and comparable business salaries for similar services.

The potential penalties and interest on any back taxes assessed by the IRS can be substantial.

An S corporation can substantially reduce taxes each year. However, other factors need to be taken into consideration to determine the amount of tax savings.

The amount of dividend distributions will change every year as the amount of profit changes. This may change the tax savings each year. You will need to estimate the amount of profit in future years to determine the tax savings.

The amount of wages subject to Social Security tax has a limit. Social Security tax is paid on wages until they reach the limit. The limit is $147,000 in 2022. The taxable maximum is based on the National Average Wage Index. The Social Security limit will be a factor for determining the best strategy.

156

In some states, S corporations are required to pay additional taxes and fees. Since it is not an S corporation it may be able to avoid paying additional state taxes and fees.

A sole proprietor may be able to pay less in total taxes by using other strategies. For example, renting from a spouse to reduce FICA taxes is a strategy a sole proprietor may be able to use.

The difference in cost of tax preparation for a sole proprietor and an S corporation should also be considered when determining the best strategy.

Changing from a sole proprietor to an S corporation can result in large tax savings each year. However, there are many factors that need to be taken into consideration to determine the best tax strategy. It may be advantageous to consult with an expert tax strategy professional to ensure that you are utilizing the best tax strategy. Many tax professionals are capable of tax preparation. However, it's crucial to find an expert in tax saving business strategies to ensure that you are saving as much money as possible.

6
BONUS STRATEGIES

Chapter 51

Tax Savings for Using Two Cars

This strategy works for single people or married people with two cars when one is primarily a business car, and the other is a personal car.

The most benefit is received if the personal car is a relatively expensive car, and it is driven a relatively small amount for personal use.

If you have two or more cars, using more than one car for business could significantly increase your business deductions without you having to spend a penny more or drive a mile further.

Example:

Scenario 1. You drive only your business car, 20,000 miles for business.

Using the mileage rate of 57.5 cents (the 2020 mileage rate) would result in a tax deduction of $11,500

Scenario 2. You drive your business car 18,000 miles for business and your personal car 2,000 miles for business. The personal car is driven a total of 4,000 miles during the year.

Your personal car cost $50,000, the insurance is $1,000/year and it gets 25 miles to the gallon.

If it's the first year your personal car is driven the depreciation rate would be 20%.

The depreciation in the first year would be $50,000 x .20 = $10,000.

Since it was used 50% for business, the allowable deductible depreciation would be $5,000. The deductible insurance would be $500. The fuel cost would be $160 (at $2.00 per gallon).

The total deduction from driving the personal car would be at least $5,660. (I haven't included any maintenance so it would be more).

The mileage deduction from driving your business car would be $10,350 (18,000 miles at 57.5).

In scenario 2, this would provide a combined deduction from both cars of $16,010 ($5,660 + $10,350).
This would result in an increase in deductions of $4,510 for the year the family car was purchased.

In the 2nd year the personal car is driven, the depreciation rate would be 32% instead of 20%. This would result in additional tax deductions of $3,000 due to the increase in the depreciation rate. ($50,000 x 12% increase in depreciation rate x 50% usage)

The total benefit in deductions would be $7,510 in the 2nd year the family car was owned.

160

Depreciation Schedule

Year	Percentage
4	20.00%
5	32.00%
6	19.20%
7	11.52%
8	11.52%
9	5.76%

Chapter 52

Deduct Sponsoring a Sports Team

If you buy uniforms, supplies or pay for other expenses such as umpires, you can deduct your expenditures. This can also include expenditures such as the cost of travel, hotels, food, gym rental and tournament fees.

Fortunately, Revenue Ruling 70-393 states that money spent to outfit and support a team is considered to be similar to money spent on other forms of advertising. The basis for this ruling is that like spending money on advertising, you hope that the expenditures to support a sports team will produce additional income.

However, if you have sponsored the team for several years without receiving any additional income, you should stop. Initially you would have grounds that you had hoped to produce additional income from sponsoring a sports team. But if you don't have any results the IRS could claim that you really had no hope of bringing in additional income and could deny the expense in later years.

Chapter 53

Avoid the IRS Classifying your Business or Farm as a Hobby

The IRS commonly examines farms and businesses to see if they can be ruled as a hobby.

If the IRS rules that your business is a hobby, the consequences can have substantial repercussions.

The consequences are even worse as a result of the 2018 tax changes. Before the 2018 tax changes, hobby income was reported on the 1040 as other income and the expenses could be deducted by itemizing on Schedule A. As a result of the tax changes the expenses are no longer deductible.

As an example of the effect of being ruled a hobby, suppose that you had previous years of losses and the IRS ruled it a hobby. In the current year, you had income of $20,000 and expenses of $19,000. If it were a business, you would pay taxes on the profit of $1,000. However, if your business is ruled a hobby, you would be paying taxes on $20,000, rather than $1,000.

If you have losses, you should be aware of the "hobby farming rules" of Internal Revenue Code Section 183, which state that the IRS won't allow you to claim any loss incurred through hobby activities as an offset against other taxable income.

For the benefit of farmers, a "two out of five years" tax rule was enacted in 1969 and revised in 1976. The regulation allows a farmer or part-time entrepreneur to elect in advance a five-year period of time in which to show the ability to make a profit.

According to the IRS, when making the distinction between a hobby or business activity, you need to consider all facts and circumstances with respect to the activity. A hobby activity is done mainly for recreation or pleasure. No one factor alone is decisive. You must generally consider these factors in determining whether an activity is a business engaged in making a profit:

- Whether you carry on the activity in a businesslike manner and maintain complete and accurate books and records.

- Whether the time and effort you put into the activity indicate you intend to make it profitable

- Whether you depend on income from the activity for your livelihood.

- Whether your losses are due to circumstances beyond your control (or are normal in the startup phase of your type of business).

- Whether you change methods of operation in an attempt to improve profitability.

- Whether you or your advisors have the knowledge

164

needed to carry on the activity as a successful business.

- Whether you were successful in making a profit in similar activities in the past.

- Whether the activity makes a profit in some years and how much profit it makes.

- Whether you can expect to make a future profit from the appreciation of the assets used in the activity.

Taking advantage of the above factors, can help your business or farm avoid being classified as a hobby. Thus, you won't have to suffer the serious tax repercussions of the IRS.

Chapter 54

Deduct your Timeshare for Business

If you use your timeshare for personal and business lodging, you may be able to deduct some of the cost as a business expense.

A business that is a sole proprietorship or a single-member LLC can claim the deduction by deducting the cost on Schedule C.

There is a different method for deducting the timeshare if your business is a corporation. If you own the timeshare personally, the corporation will need to reimburse you for your expenses and depreciation as employee business expenses. Your corporation reimbursement should follow the rules of an accountable plan in order to keep you from reporting the payment as income.

Timeshares can be purchased as either deeded or non-deeded.

If you bought a deeded timeshare, you would have an ownership interest in the real estate. In this case you would allocate the purchase price to land, land improvements, building and personal property.

The building would be depreciated over 39 years since it is being rented for commercial use of business lodging property. You would write off the interest if it was being

166

financed. Annual maintenance fees would be deducted as lodging expenses.

The other type of purchase is a non-deeded timeshare, where you buy a lease, license or club membership that lets you use the property for a set amount of time each year for an agreed upon number of years.

With the non-deeded property, you would allocate the cost over the number of years of the lease. You would also deduct the annual maintenance fee each year if there was one.

If you use the timeshare for business and personal purposes during the year, you simply allocate the costs between personal, and business uses. As an example, if you used the timeshare one week for business and one week for personal use you would be able to deduct 50% of the cost as a business expense.

Don't rent the timeshare if you want to receive the maximum tax benefits from your timeshare. If you rent your timeshare, it complicates your tax-deduction. Although you can still receive some benefits.

By not renting it you can avoid the vacation-home rules that limit deductions. However, there is an exception if you rent to relatives.

Fortunately, the tax laws allow you to rent the timeshare at fair market rent to a relative. Your relative's rental of the timeshare counts as personal use by you. Your relative could even write you a check and you could deposit it in the bank without creating any additional tax issues. For this purpose, relatives include your immediate family which would be your parents, brothers and sisters, children and grandparents.

Bringing a business associate along with you to your timeshare is a great way for you to provide a free vacation location for them and a tax write off for you. And of course, it will provide an opportunity to discuss business and develop your relationship.

Chapter 55

Deduct Your Motorhome

If you have a business and use a motor home, it's important to know the IRS rules for deducting it for business.

The IRS classifies a motorhome in one of two ways. Depending on your circumstances it's either a business transportation vehicle or a business lodging facility.

The IRS and the courts have had trouble trying to determine when the motorhome is a business lodging facility or a business vehicle.

The court has decided that deciding the primary use requires finding a common denominator and then measuring the result.

When measuring the primary use of a vehicle, you keep a record of business and personal miles. For example, if you drove 15,000 miles for business and 5,000 personal miles, you would have 75% business use.

When measuring primary use of a lodging facility, you keep a record of the number of business nights and personal nights.

Since the IRS has trouble deciding how a motor home is classified, you should keep track of both mileage and nights.

The IRS rules normally allow you to deduct the entire cost of large vehicles in the first year or depreciate it over 5 years. If you expense an asset in the first year you are required to take the Section 179 deduction. The problem with taking the Section 179 deduction is that you must report the type of asset. When the IRS sees that a motor home is being deducted, your return has an increased chance of being audited.

Another problem with taking the Section 179 deduction is that if the motor home is ruled a lodging facility, it is not eligible for the Section 179 deduction.

Do not use your motor home as an entertainment facility either directly or indirectly. Direct use would include having people over for a party. Indirect use would include driving it to your hunting area.
The tax code allows no deduction for any facility used in connection with entertainment.

Your motor home should be used over 50% as a means of transportation as long as you are depreciating it. If you can't claim the "more than 50%" test during this period, you will have to pay taxes when you sell it. You will be required to pay taxes at ordinary income rates on the recapture of some of your prior depreciation.

If the IRS decides that your motor home is lavish and extravagant, your depreciation will not be allowed.

However, this is somewhat of a gray area. For example, if you are a doctor or an attorney the IRS is less likely to classify it as lavish and extravagant than if you were

170

using it for construction.

It is extremely important to keep good records in the event of an audit. Record your mileage every time you use it for business and personal use. Be sure that it has more than 50% business miles for the year. Record every night that it is used for business or personal lodging. Be sure that more than 50% were business nights for the year.

Chapter 56

Deduct Your Cabin or Beach House

Your vacation home can provide a huge tax deduction while also allowing the home to be used for vacations.

Having a vacation home that is used for business allows you to claim a deduction for mortgage interest, property taxes, homeowners' insurance, HOA fees, utilities, refuse, repairs, and depreciation of the building, remodeling, and assets.

According to Section 280A(f)(4) of the tax code, personal use of a home doesn't disallow the business expenses for travel away from home. However, it is crucial to understand the tax laws.

It's important to avoid using the property for entertainment. As a result of the Tax Cuts and Jobs Act (TCJA), business entertainment is no longer tax-deductible. In the Ireland court case, any use of a beach home for entertainment eliminates any deduction when there is any entertainment. Never use your property for entertainment purposes.

If you use a second home only for business and personal use, the deductible expense is determined by the percentage of lodging that was used for the business.

Be sure you know the tax home rules.

172

If you rent your vacation home, you can trigger the vacation-home rules which makes your scenario much more complicated. Renting can trigger the following vacation-home rules:

- A split between the rental and personal-use deductions.

- Classification of your vacation home as either a personal residence or rental property.

- A loss of tax-favored hotel status for qualified rentals.

- Passive-loss rules that defer current tax benefits to future years.

If you use your second home solely for business lodging, you escape the vacation-home rules. The property is treated as a 100% business asset and completely deductible. Keep in mind that none of the business use can be for entertainment.

It's important to create proof of your property's use. You need to prove how many nights you slept in your vacation property for both personal and business purposes. Keep any third-party evidence as proof. This includes email, letters, and other proof of why you traveled there. Receipts for fuel, groceries, and restaurants will provide evidence that you were in the area.

If your business is taxed as a sole proprietorship or an LLC, deduct the business percentage as business expenses on your Schedule C.

If your business is a corporation, submit an expense report to the corporation for reimbursement.

There is one exception to the business lodging rule. Landlords who rent dwelling units can't deduct staying at a vacation rental to take care of the rental units.

It's critical to know what qualifies as business days.

You must work at least 4 hours to be considered a business day. However, if your presence is required at a particular place for a specific business purpose, the day is a business day no matter how much time was spent on business.

The day qualifies as a business day even If you travel with the intention of a business purpose but could not conduct business because of circumstances beyond your control.

Travel days also count as business days as long as you use a reasonably direct route.

Weekends and holidays count as business days if it's not cost-effective to go home for the weekend.

In addition to deducting your vacation home, a business day also enables you to deduct food for the day.

174

Conclusion

Tax-saving business strategies can substantially reduce the amount of taxes paid by a business.

This book is intended to provide 56 of my favorite business tax-saving strategies. You may be able to save a significant amount of money by using one or several of the book's strategies. The strategies should be thoroughly researched before implementing them. Also, there are several other strategies that could benefit your business. There are additional perks of creating strategies to deduct travel and vacations. In order to determine the best tax-saving business strategies, it is important to consult your business tax-strategy expert every year.

It is important to be proactive with tax planning for your business. I recommend that you review your strategies with your tax expert every year, especially if you have a fast-growing business. Also, there are changes to tax laws every year that could impact the strategies you use.

For example, I have had many new business clients who have either prepared their own taxes or went to a large national tax company to prepare their tax returns to save money or for convenience. Most have never spoken with a business tax-strategy expert. I have been able to amend their tax returns and save them thousands of dollars for a fee that was a small percentage of their tax savings. Amending returns only provides savings for that year. I have been able to provide these clients with strategies that save them money for future years.

Additionally, I have prepared taxes for clients who thought they had a tax professional who was an expert with tax strategies. I would ask them how many strategies their tax professional discussed with them and was shocked to learn that it was either none or very few. After talking to these clients and asking them the correct questions about their business, I have been able to create strategies and find missed deductions that save them thousands of dollars each year. Unfortunately, if these clients had come to me sooner, they would have been able to save thousands of dollars in previous years as well.

I hope this book provided you with valuable information for your business that was easy to understand.

It's your money, keep it or give it to the IRS!

Additional tax strategies, tax news, and valuable information are available on my videos, radio shows, and newspaper columns at YourTaxCare.com.

I am available to answer your questions about tax-saving strategies or tax problems. I can be emailed at David@YourTaxCare.com or be reached by call or text at (865) 221-7477.

About the Author

David C. Zubler is an Enrolled Agent. Enrolled Agent status is the highest credential the IRS awards. Enrolled Agents, like attorneys, have unlimited practice rights in tax representation before the IRS. He graduated from Penn State in accounting and Pellissippi State in computer science with high distinction. David has studied with the Bradford Tax Institute, American Society of Tax Problem Solvers, National Association of Tax Professionals and Michael Rozbruch's Tax & Business Solutions Academy to further his expertise in solving IRS tax problems.

As a result of the increased demand for his services, David has formed Your Tax Care and has staffed his office to meet his client's tax needs. Your Tax Care specializes in painless and permanent rescues for people with tax problems.

Your Tax Care was also created to provide tax education and news at YourTaxCare.com.

David has three daughters and nine grandchildren. When not helping his clients with tax solutions, he enjoys adventure, the outdoors, travel, and linguistics. He has studied and speaks Spanish, French, and Italian. He enjoys travel and vacationing and doing many types of fun activities with his family, friends, and clients.

David's other books include:

Great Tax Tips

& Valuable Information For The Tax Challenged

Simplifying The 2018 Tax Changes

And How It Affects You

How To Beat The IRS

With Tax Saving Business Strategies

Fight the IRS And Win

Secrets of An Enrolled Agent

Trucking Tax Saving Strategies

How to Create Your Success

The books are available on Amazon or at YourTaxCare.com

THE IDEAL PROFESSIONAL SPEAKER FOR YOUR NEXT EVENT!

Help business owners achieve greater success.

Any organization that wants to increase knowledge and success needs to hire David for a keynote and/or workshop training!

TO CONTACT OR BOOK DAVID FOR YOUR NEXT EVENT:

David Zubler
9041 Executive Park Dr
Suite A202
Knoxville, TN 37923

(865) 221-7477

David@YourTaxCare.com

Made in the USA
Columbia, SC
12 July 2022

63301487R00108